Unlocking Social Studies Skills

John R. O'Connor

Robert M. Goldberg

Globe Book Company

New York/Cleveland/Toronto

John R. O'Connor
B.A., St. Francis College
M.A., University of Pittsburgh

Mr. O'Connor taught social studies for many years before becoming a principal in the New York City school system. He is widely known for his lectures and articles on reading skills in the social studies. Mr. O'Connor co-authored the textbooks *Exploring World History*, *Exploring the Urban World*, *Exploring Urban New York*, and *Exploring American Citizenship*. In addition to this textbook, he has edited *Exploring the Non-Western World*, *Exploring the Western World*, *Exploring Africa, South of the Sahara*, and *The New Exploring American History*.

Robert M. Goldberg

Mr. Goldberg is a social studies specialist, active in the field of urban education and especially interested in remedial reading. He is a member of the National Council for the Social Studies and was formerly Educational Consultant for Diagnostic, Prescriptive, and Remediation Teaching in Oceanside, New York. He is currently chairman of the Social Studies Department in a junior high school in Oceanside, New York. Mr. Goldberg is co-author of *Exploring Urban New York*, *Exploring the Urban World*, and *Exploring American Citizenship*.

Editorial, design, and production assistance: Christine Reynolds, The Book Department, Inc.
Technical illustrations: Deborah Schneck
Map art: Richard Sanderson
Cover design: Greg Johnson, The Book Department, Inc.
Photo acknowledgments: Pages 1, 32, 92, and title page, Cymie Payne; Page 62, Stock Boston.

Second Edition 1985

ISBN: 0-87065-585-X

PRINTED IN THE UNITED STATES OF AMERICA
7   8   9   10   11   12

Table of Contents

UNIT 1
Map Skills

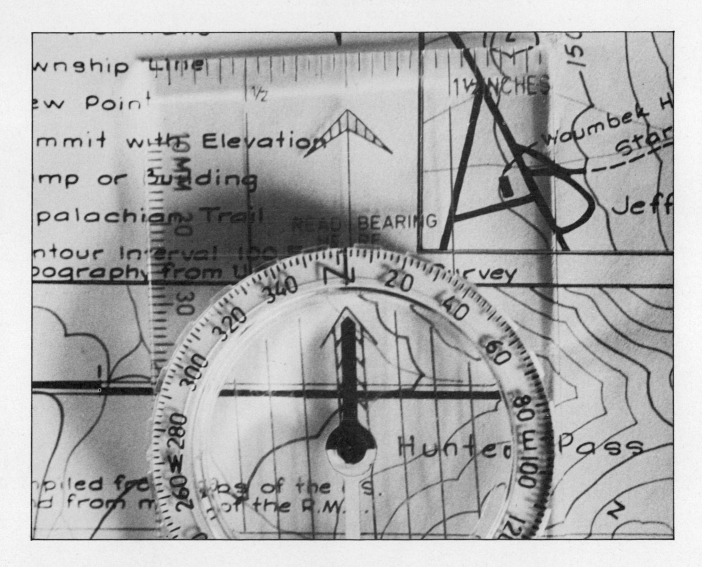

1. Telling Directions

Lesson 1 will show you how to:
- Locate a place on a map by following directions.
- Choose the direction to travel when you want to go from one place to another.

Direction is one of the main things a map shows us. There are four basic directions: north, south, east, and west. North means the direction toward the North Pole. South means toward the South Pole. The poles are places located at opposite ends of the earth's axis. The axis is an imaginary line running through the earth.

Most maps will have north at the top. But this is not always so. North can be at the top, the bottom, or either side of a map, depending on the way the map is drawn.

To find out where north and other directions are on a map, check the *direction finder*. On most maps the direction finder looks like this:

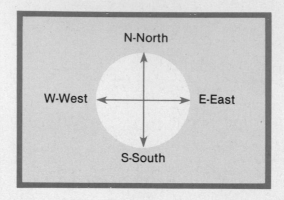

Suppose you do not see such a diagram on a map. Then you can assume that the direction north is at the top of the map.

Of course, places are not always directly north, south, east, or west of each other. There are in-between places. The complete diagram of directions, then, looks like this:

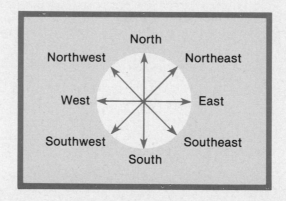

So, in addition to north, south, east, and west, this direction finder tells us:

1. Northeast is in the direction halfway between north and east.
2. Southeast is in the direction halfway between south and east.
3. Northwest is in the direction halfway between north and west.
4. Southwest is in the direction halfway between south and west.

A direction finder is also called a *compass rose*. Can you figure out why?

FOLLOW THE LINES

A. Here is a diagram with the names of make-believe towns. Each town is located on a line of the direction finder. But the names of the directions are not shown.

Use this diagram and the direction finder on the preceding page to tell in which direction these make-believe towns are from each other. Write the correct direction in the blanks below. The first one has been done for you.

1. Rake is ___South___ of Top.

2. Sock is _____ of Salt.

3. Root is _____ of Wade.

4. Back is _____ of Boat.

5. Top is _____ of Rake.

6. Wade is_____ of Root.

7. Salt is _____ of Sock.

8. Boat is _____ of Back.

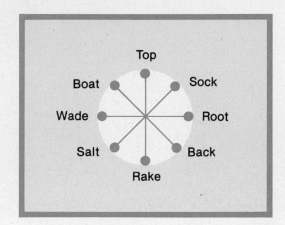

B. Follow the zigzag lines and figure out in which direction you are traveling as you go from one letter to the next. Use the *compass rose* as a help. Write the correct direction in each blank below. The first one has been done for you.

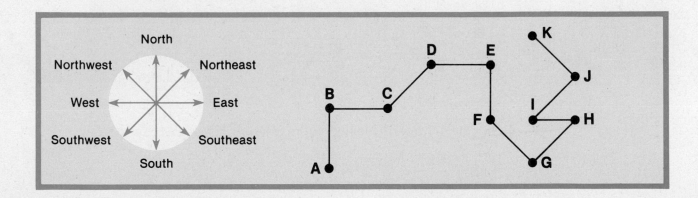

1. To get from A to B, travel __north__.

2. To get from B to C, travel _____.

3. To get from C to D, travel _____.

4. To get from D to E, travel _____.

5. To get from E to F, travel _____.

6. To get from F to G, travel _____.

7. To get from G to H, travel _____.

8. To get from H to I, travel _____.

9. To get from I to J, travel _____.

10. To get from J to K, travel _____.

WHICH DIRECTION IS IT?

Use the direction finder and the map of North America below to fill in the blanks that follow. Read each statement or question. Then write your answer in the blank.

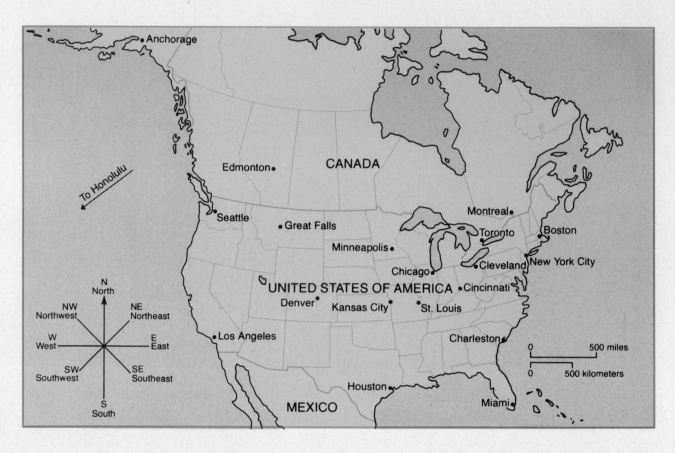

1. The city of _____ is almost directly south of Kansas City.

2. The city of _____ is almost directly east of Seattle.

3. St. Louis is almost directly _____ of Kansas City.

4. In which direction would you be traveling if you went by airplane from

   a. Denver to Minneapolis? _____

   b. Chicago to Cleveland? _____

   c. Houston to Kansas City? _____

   d. New York to Toronto? _____

   e. Los Angeles to Seattle? _____

   f. Charleston to Boston? _____

   g. Seattle to Anchorage? _____

   h. Kansas City to Great Falls? _____

2. Directions and Places

Lesson 2 will show you how to:
- Find specific places on a simple street map.

On page 7 is a map of the town of Post. It shows all the main roads of the town. Notice how they are named. All those running in an east and west direction are called *avenues*. All those running north and south are called *streets*.

Find Central Avenue on the map. Do you see that it runs east and west through the center of Post? Next, find Main Street. It runs through the center of Post, too. But it goes in a different direction—north and south.

THE ROADS OF POST

A. Locate all the *avenues* of Post on the map. Write their names in the following spaces.

1. _____

2. _____

3. _____

4. _____

5. _____

6. _____

7. _____

8. _____

9. _____

B. Locate all the *streets* of Post on the map. Write their names in the following spaces.

1. _____

2. _____

3. _____

4. _____

5. _____

6. _____

7. _____

FINDING PLACES IN POST

Look at the map of Post again. Study the streets of the town. Notice how they are named and numbered east and west of Main Street. Next, study the avenues of Post. Notice how they are named and numbered north and south of Central Avenue. Now complete the exercises that follow.

A. Use the map of Post to find the street or avenue that answers each question. Write the name of the street or avenue in the space provided.

1. Which avenue is directly north of First Avenue North? _____

2. Which avenue is directly south of Second Avenue South? _____

3. What is the first street east of Main Street? _____

4. What is the street directly west of Second Street West? _____

5. Which avenue is directly south of Fourth Avenue North? _____

6. Which street is directly east of First Street West? _____

B. Use the map to find the places where the streets and avenues of Post cross each other.

1. Write on the map the number 1 where First Street East and Central Avenue cross.

2. Write the number 2 where First Street East and First Avenue North cross.

3. Write the number 3 where Second Street East and Second Avenue North cross.

4. Write the number 4 where Third Street East and Second Avenue South cross.

5. Write the number 5 where Second Street West and Third Avenue North cross.

6. Write the number 6 where Central Avenue and Third Street West cross.

7. Write the letter A where First Avenue South and First Street West cross.

8. Write the letter B where Third Avenue South and First Street East cross.

9. Write the letter C where Second Avenue North and Third Street West cross.

10. Write the letter D where Fourth Avenue North and Second Street East cross.

11. Write the letter E where Central Avenue and Third Street East cross.

12. Write the letter O at the southeast corner of Central Avenue and Main Street.

13. Write the letter Y at the northeast corner of Central Avenue and Main Street.

14. Write the letter Z at the southwest corner of Third Avenue South and Third Street West.

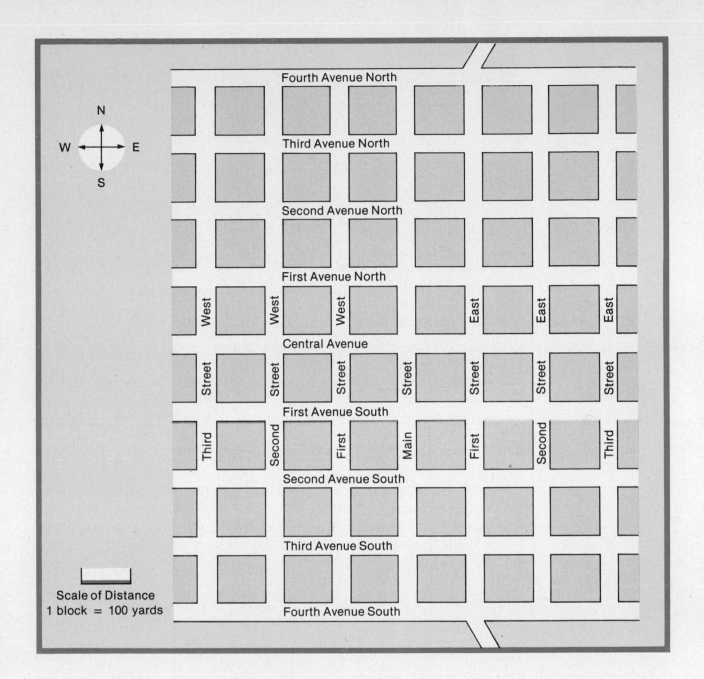

Fourth Avenue North

Third Avenue North

Second Avenue North

First Avenue North

Central Avenue

First Avenue South

Second Avenue South

Third Avenue South

Fourth Avenue South

N
W — E
S

West Street
West Street
West Street
East Street
East Street
East Street

Third Street
Second Street
First Street
Main Street
First Street
Second Street
Third Street

Scale of Distance
1 block = 100 yards

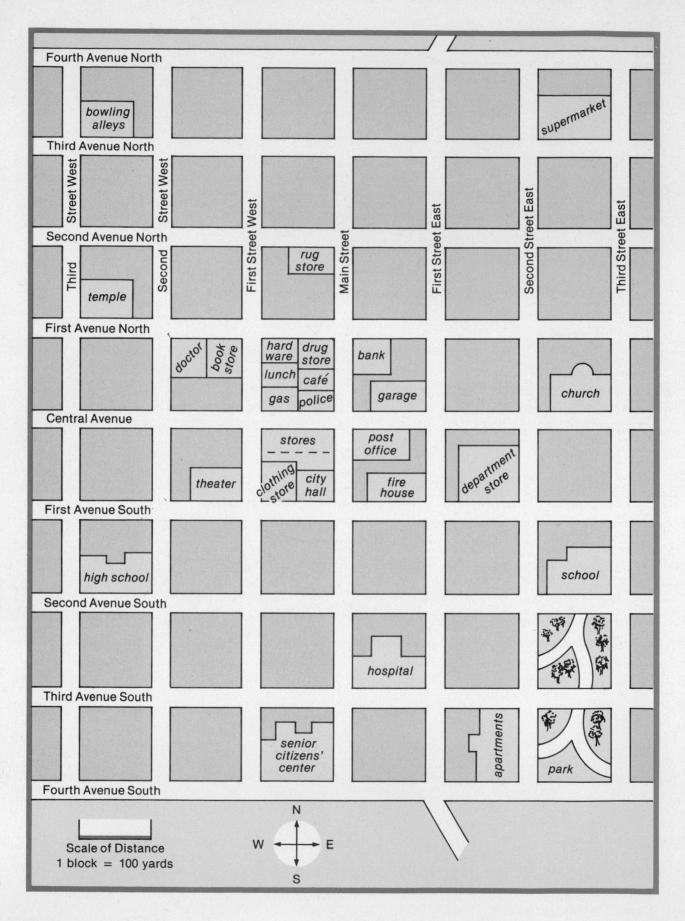

Fourth Avenue North

bowling alleys

Third Avenue North

Street West

Street West

Second Avenue North

Third

Second

First Street West

Main Street

First Street East

Second Street East

Third Street East

rug store

temple

supermarket

First Avenue North

doctor

book store

hard ware

drug store

lunch

café

gas

police

bank

garage

church

Central Avenue

stores

clothing store

city hall

post office

fire house

department store

theater

First Avenue South

high school

school

Second Avenue South

hospital

Third Avenue South

senior citizens' center

apartments

park

Fourth Avenue South

Scale of Distance
1 block = 100 yards

N
W — E
S

3. Using Directions to Locate Places

At left is another map of the town of Post. This map shows not only the streets and avenues of Post, but many other places as well—for example, the fire house, the bank, the department store, the school, and the hospital. With the map you can locate places in Post, and you can make some educated guesses about life in the town.

MORE ABOUT POST

Study the map of Post. Then use the map to answer the following questions. Write the correct letter in the space provided.

1. Which of these buildings is located directly south of the bookstore?

   _____

   a. post office   b. theater   c. city hall   d. high school

2. Which of these buildings is located on the same block as the city hall?

   _____

   a. fire house   b. theater   c. bank   d. clothing store

3. Where is the doctor's office located? _____
   a. at the corner of First Avenue North and Second Street West
   b. across the street from the hardware store
   c. on Central Avenue
   d. east of Main Street

4. If you walked from the bank to the high school, how far would you have

   to go? _____
   a. 3 blocks   b. 4 blocks   c. 5 blocks   d. 7 blocks

5. Fred lives three blocks north of the department store. So, Fred's home is

   located _____.
   a. at Second Avenue North and Main Street
   b. at Third Avenue North and Second Street East
   c. east of the supermarket
   d. directly north of the bank

6. All of the following buildings are located on Central Avenue except the

   _____.

   a. church   b. police station   c. post office   d. bank

7. If you walked from the drug store to the park, you would travel _____.
   a. south, then west   c. west, then south
   b. south, then east   d. east, then north

8. Probably, the quietest street in Post is _____.
   a. Third Avenue South   c. Central Avenue
   b. First Avenue South   d. First Street West

9. The street that probably has the most traffic and the most activity during

   the day is _____.
   a. Third Avenue North   c. First Street East
   b. Main Street   d. Second Street West

10. If you walked from one end of Post to the other in a north-south direc-

    tion, you would travel nearly _____.
    a. 400 yards   b. 800 yards   c. 1,200 yards   d. 1,600 yards

11. A home located on _____ would be nearest to the park.
    a. First Avenue South and Second Street West
    b. Second Avenue South and Third Street East
    c. Central Avenue and Main Street
    d. First Avenue North and Second Street East

12. If a visitor to Post asked you where the "center of town" was located, you

    would be right to direct him or her to the _____.
    a. corner with the bank   b. theater   c. post office   d. fire house

13. Which building is located at each of the following places:
    a. southeast corner of First Avenue North and Main Street?

    _____

    b. northeast corner of Central Avenue and First Street West?

    _____

    c. northwest corner of Central Avenue and Main Street?

    _____

    d. southwest corner of First Avenue North and First Street West?

    _____

10

4. Using the Scale of Distance

Lesson 4 will show you how to:
- Use a scale to measure distances on a simple road map.
- Get information about the map from the legend, or key.

HOW DOES A MAP WORK?

Maps are pictures of the earth. A map can show a country, a state, or a city. Maps come in different sizes. The whole world can be shown on one page in a book. Or a map of a city street could cover a whole classroom wall.

Maps can show things we can see and things we cannot see. For instance, a map can show the location of mountains, lakes, rivers, cities, and buildings. It can also picture invisible things like the boundaries separating one country from another, the number of languages spoken in one part of the world, or the amount of rain that falls in one year in a place.

The first part of reading a map is to find out what the map shows. Look for the title of the map. Then look at all the places and things named on the map.

Next, find the map's legend, or key. It is usually placed in a corner of the map. The legend will give you all the symbols that are used on the map to show things about the earth. The symbols used on a map are a kind of shorthand. They can tell us many things quickly that might take many pages to read about.

Most maps use the color blue to stand for bodies of water on the earth. Lines—either solid or dashed—are usually used to stand for the boundaries of countries and states. In this lesson, dots are used to stand for whole towns.

The legend also has a scale of distance. The scale tells you what distances on the map stand for. One inch on the map, for example, can stand for one mile on the earth. Or, the scale might tell you that two inches on the map stands for a distance of two hundred miles on the earth.

If the scale is a metric scale, it will tell you what each centimeter on the map stands for. A centimeter may, for instance, stand for 1 kilometer, 100 kilometers, or 500 kilometers. Many scales of distance give both miles and kilometers.

TRY IT OUT

Take out an index card or a piece of cardboard and measure each of the three scales of miles shown in this exercise. See how long each scale is and mark off the length on your card. Use a different edge of the card for each scale. With each of your scales complete the three exercises that follow. Measure the most direct distance between dots without passing through other dots if possible.

A. The scale of distance for this exercise is: | 1 Mile |
1 Inch = 1 Mile

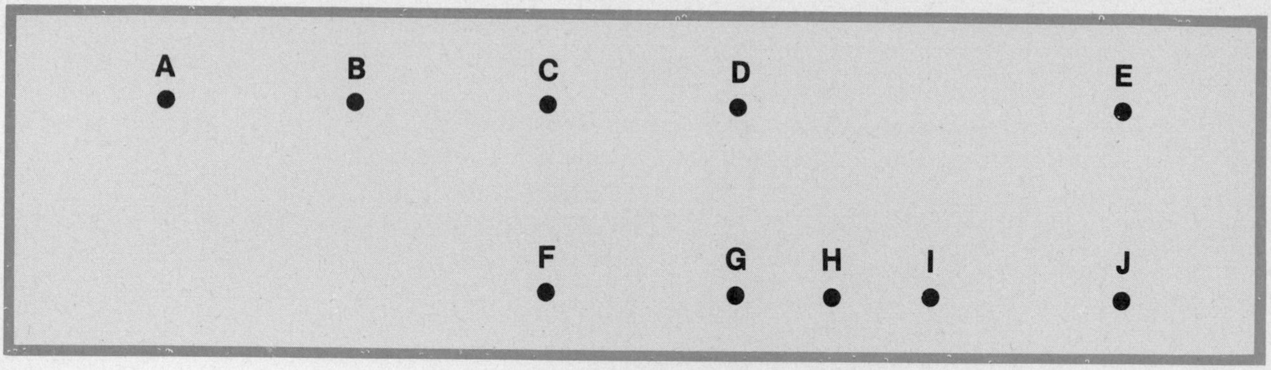

A ●   B ●   C ●   D ●   E ●

F ●   G ●   H ●   I ●   J ●

Using the scale of distance, how far is it between the dots?

A to B _____	F to I _____	A to E _____
A to C _____	F to H _____	A to J _____
A to D _____	G to H _____	C to I _____
D to F _____	D to H _____	C to H _____
D to E _____	A to H _____	B to J _____

B. The scale of distance for this exercise is: | 2 Miles |
1 Inch = 2 Miles

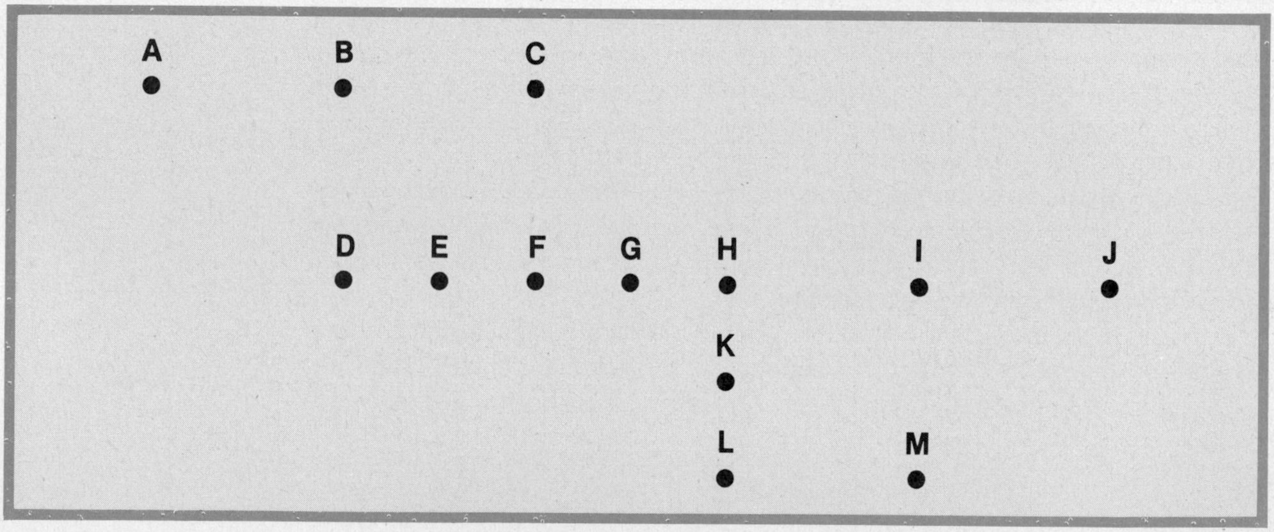

A ●   B ●   C ●

D ●   E ●   F ●   G ●   H ●   I ●   J ●

K ●

L ●   M ●

How far is it between the dots?

A to B _____	C to F _____	D to J _____
A to C _____	C to G _____	C to I _____
A to D _____	D to G _____	B to F _____
A to E _____	F to G _____	B to J _____

C. The scale of distance for this exercise is:

| 1½ Miles |

1 Inch = 1½ Miles

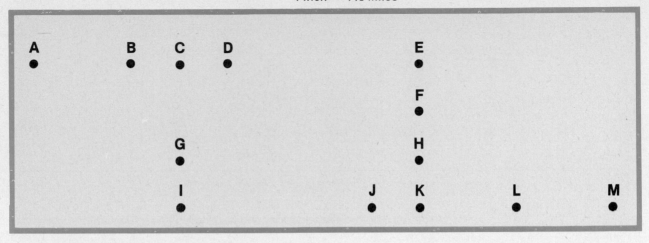

How far is it between the dots?

A to B _____   A to F _____   B to J _____

A to I _____   E to K _____   C to L _____

A to C _____   E to M _____   F to I _____

A to D _____   D to M _____   G to E _____

D. Of course, real places are not as evenly spaced as the dots were spaced in the exercises you have just completed. And the roads connecting places are not always straight. The map below shows towns connected by roads. Use your ruler to tell the distances between the towns. If you do not have a ruler, use an index card, a piece of cardboard, or a piece of paper. Mark off the length of the scale of distance on the card or paper.

It is not always possible to tell the *exact* distance between places on a map. But you can be very accurate if you "bend" your ruler or card to follow the roads as closely as possible.

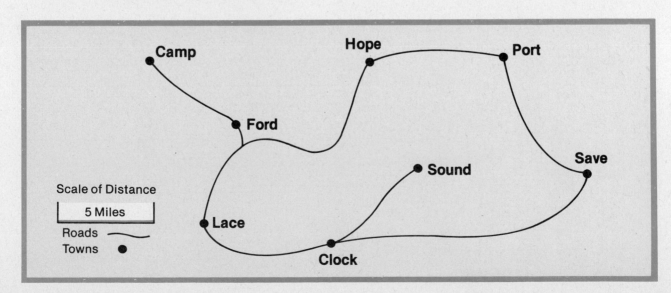

The distance by car from:

Camp to Ford is about _____ miles.   Camp to Lace is about _____ miles.

Ford to Hope is about _____ miles.   Clock to Sound is about _____ miles.

Hope to Port is about _____ miles.   Lace to Sound is about _____ miles.

Hope to Save is about _____ miles.   Lace to Save is about _____ miles.

Save to Clock is about _____ miles.   Hope to Lace is about _____ miles.

The distance by air from Camp to Save is about _____ miles.

REVIEWING DIRECTION AND DISTANCE

Study the map below. Read the legend carefully. Then answer the questions that follow.

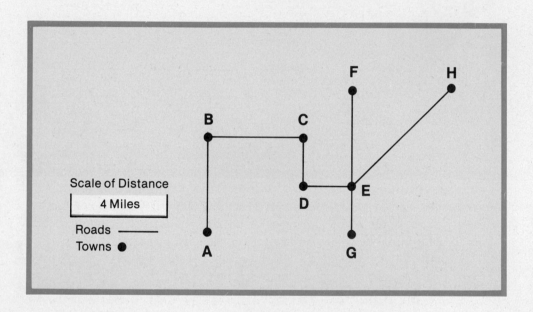

1. What direction would you travel if you went from E to H? _____

2. From F to G? _____

3. From G to B? _____

4. How far would you travel in miles if you went by car from B to G?

   _____

5. From A to H? _____

6. How far is it from A to H by air? _____

5. Reading a Map of More than One Place

Lesson 5 will show you how to:
- Read the symbols on a legend, or key.
- Recognize that a particular place will not always appear the same size on every map.

Look back at the map of Post in Lesson 3. Notice that the whole map pictures the town of Post. It gives a close-up view of Post's streets, avenues, and buildings. There is nothing on the map except Post.

Now look at the map on page 17. This map shows not only Post but also the area around it. Located in this area is the much larger town of Lock. In fact, Lock takes up most of the space on this map.

Because the map shows two different-sized towns—one large and one much smaller—the ways the towns are pictured differ. Lock, the large town, is shown by a large square. A much smaller square stands for the smaller town of Post. By doing this, we can show how the sizes of the towns compare.

To show many things about one place we use a map like the one of Post in Lesson 3. But to show several places—some in more detail than others—we use maps like this one.

READING A MAP

Study the map of Post and the area around it. Pay special attention to the legend, or key, in the corner of the map. It will enable you to "read" the numbers and symbols on the map correctly. Then choose the best answer for each question. Write the correct letter in the space provided.

_____ 1. Only one street in Post is shown on the map because

    a. Highway 7 is the only street in Post.
    b. Post is too small on the map to show all the streets.
    c. the streets of Post are not numbered.

_____ 2. Highway 7 in Post is shown on the map because it

    a. is an important road that also goes through Lock.
    b. is the only state highway shown on the map.
    c. runs in a north-south direction.

_____ 3. The town of Lock is about

    a. 6 miles long and 3 miles wide.
    b. 3 miles long and 3 miles wide.
    c. 6 miles long and 6 miles wide.

_____ 4. If you entered Lock from Highway 3 on the north and continued on Highway 3 through the town, you would

    a. go south on First Avenue, then east on Main Street.

    b. go south on First Avenue, east to Ohio Avenue, then south.

    c. go south on Main Street, then east on Ohio Avenue.

_____ 5. If you were telling a traveler by car how to go from Post to Highway 10, you would tell her or him to

    a. follow Highway 7 to Park Street, then drive east past Ohio Avenue.

    b. follow Highway 7 east to Oak Street, then drive south and east on Park Street.

    c. follow Highway 7 south on Lincoln Avenue, then drive west on Park Street.

_____ 6. If you have entered Lock from Highway 10 and want to get to Lake Ness by the most direct route, you should follow

    a. Park Street to Ohio Avenue, then go north on Highway 3.

    b. Park Street to Lincoln Avenue, then go north to Main Street, west to Highway 3, and north again.

    c. Park Street east to First Avenue, then go north on Highway 3.

_____ 7. The distance from Post to Lock is approximately

    a. 1 mile.   b. 2½ miles.   c. 3½ miles.   d. 4 miles.

_____ 8. The distance from Park Street and First Avenue in Lock to the entrance to Lake Ness is about

    a. 3 miles.   b. 5½ miles.   c. 6 miles.   d. 7½ miles.

_____ 9. The distance around Lock is about

    a. twice the distance around Post.

    b. six miles.

    c. five times the distance around Post.

    d. the length of Route 7 on the map.

_____ 10. Swamp Road does not have a number because it

    a. is not a state highway.

    b. does not connect with a state highway.

    c. does not go through a town.

_____ 11. Which of these streets in Lock would probably have the most automobile traffic?

    a. Maple Street   c. Ohio Avenue

    b. Pearl Street   d. First Avenue

_____ 12. At which of these locations in Lock might a gas station get the most business?

    a. where Maple Street crosses Ohio Avenue

    b. where Main Street crosses Lincoln Avenue

    c. where Madison Street crosses First Avenue

13. Which of the three state highways shown on the map begins at Lock?

   a. Highway 3
   b. Highway 7
   c. Highway 10

14. Which of the following is the best description of how Highway 7 appears on the map?

   a. enters Lock from the south, runs north through the town, then west and north through Post
   b. enters Lock from the southwest, runs north through Lock, then west through Post
   c. enters Lock from the east, and continues north

15. Which of the following is the best description of how Highway 3 appears on the map?

   a. enters Lock from the north, continues south to Main Street, then runs east and southeast after leaving Lock
   b. enters Lock from the south, then runs west on Main Street
   c. enters Lock from the east, continues east on Main Street, runs north through Lock, and then continues northwest

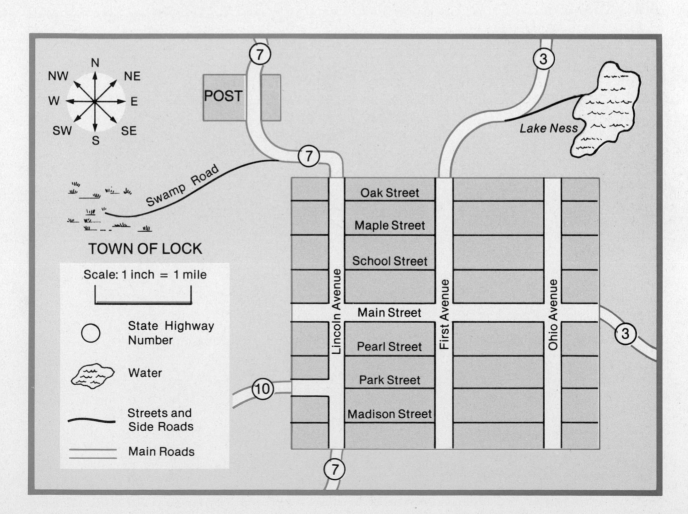

TOWN OF LOCK

Scale: 1 inch = 1 mile

State Highway Number

Water

Streets and Side Roads

Main Roads

6. Reading a Map of a State

Lesson 6 will show you how to:
- Practice what you have already learned about maps.
- Read a map of a typical state.
- Learn to draw conclusions from information on a map.

Below is a map of the state of Futura. Futura covers a large area. As you can see, the towns of Post and Lock are located in Futura. On the map in Lesson 5, Post and Lock were a big part of a small area. So, they were shown by squares. On the map of Futura, the towns are a small part of a large area. So, they are shown by dots.

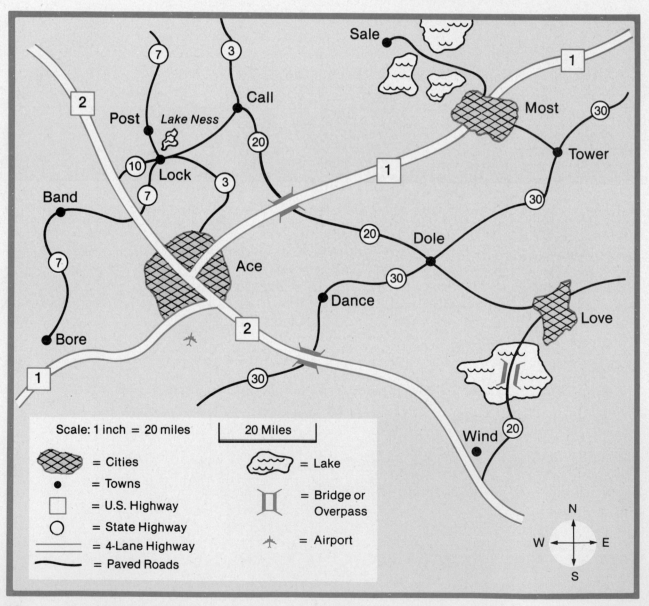

By studying the map of Futura, we can learn many things about a large area. For instance, we can see that the state has more than one kind of community. Futura has cities as well as towns. To show many things about a place, a map must use many different symbols. On the legend of this map you will see symbols you already know, as well as new ones. With the symbols you can draw conclusions about the state of Futura.

FINDING OUT ABOUT FUTURA

Study the map of Futura. Pay special attention to the symbols used to tell us about the state. Then answer the following questions. Write the correct letter in the space provided.

1. The size of the state of Futura, measured from east to west, is about

   _____.

   a. 80 miles
   b. 100 miles
   c. 120 miles
   d. 140 miles

2. In which part of Futura are Post and Lock located? _____

   a. northwest
   b. northeast
   c. the center
   d. north

3. How many cities are located in the state of Futura? _____

   a. one
   b. two
   c. three
   d. four

4. The largest city in the state is _____.

   a. Most
   b. Love
   c. Ace
   d. Dole

5. According to the information on the map, which of the following statements is the most accurate? _____

   a. Lock is larger than Call.
   b. Lock is smaller than Tower.
   c. Lock has more people than Wind.
   d. Lock is probably the same size as Dance.

6. How many United States Highways are there in Futura? _____

   a. one
   b. two
   c. three
   d. four

7. Which United States Highway runs from northeast to southwest through
Futura? _____
   a. Highway 1
   b. Highway 2
   c. Highway 3
   d. Highway 20

8. The two most important highway routes in Futura are _____.
   a. Highways 20 and 30
   b. Highways 1 and 2
   c. Highways 3 and 7
   d. Highways 3 and 10

9. The shortest distance from Tower to Most is about _____.
   a. 12 miles
   b. 23 miles
   c. 30 miles
   d. 42 miles

10. In driving the shortest distance from Love to Ace, you would go through

   _____.
   a. Wind
   b. Dole
   c. Dance
   d. Tower

11. A vacation or recreation area would probably be located near _____.
   a. Tower
   b. Band
   c. Sale
   d. Dole

12. The largest number of gas stations would probably be found in _____.
   a. Dance
   b. Post
   c. Dole
   d. Band

13. You might see a sign that says, "ACE—20 MILES," in _____.
   a. Dole
   b. Band
   c. Lock
   d. Call

14. The shortest distance by car from Love to Wind would be almost _____.
   a. 20 miles
   b. 40 miles
   c. 60 miles
   d. 80 miles

15. In going from Ace to Wind, you would travel _____.
    a. northwest
    b. northeast
    c. southwest
    d. southeast

16. You would pass over a bridge in driving from _____.
    a. Sale to Ace
    b. Most to Sale
    c. Dance to Tower
    d. Lock to Ace

17. Each of these is located on Highway 30 except _____.
    a. Most
    b. Tower
    c. Dance
    d. Dole

18. Each of these towns is located at a *crossroads* (where two roads meet) except _____.
    a. Love
    b. Lock
    c. Call
    d. Dance

19. Which of the following towns is located on both Highways 1 and 2?

    _____
    a. Ace
    b. Most
    c. Wind
    d. Bore

20. Highways 3, 7, and 10 pass through _____.
    a. Call
    b. Ace
    c. Post
    d. Lock

21. An airport is located near _____.
    a. Band
    b. Ace
    c. Lock
    d. Dole

7. Landforms

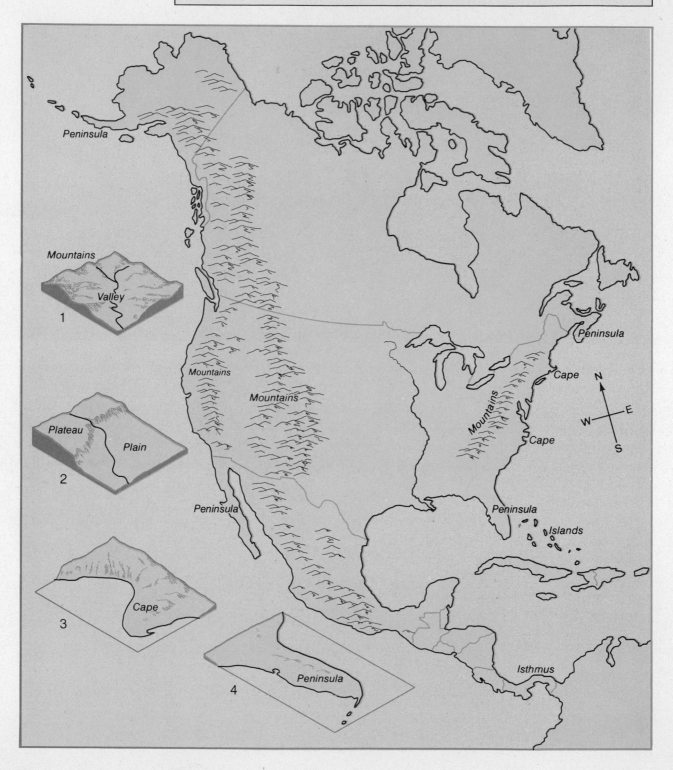

22

The earth's surface has many different shapes. Some shapes, like hills and mountains, rise high above the ground. Others, like plains, are low and level. Between hills and mountains we find another shape—the valley. In the middle of a body of water, we can find still another—an island.

We call these different shapes *landforms*. The largest landform on the earth's surface is the *continent*. North and South America, Asia, Africa, Europe, and Australia are continents. Some geographers also call Antarctica a continent. Other important landforms include the following:

Cape: a piece of land stretching out into the sea.

Coastline: land along a very large body of water such as an ocean.

Island: land entirely surrounded by water.

Isthmus: a narrow strip of land joining two larger land areas.

Mountains: a landform that rises at least 1,000 feet above the land surrounding it.

Peninsula: a piece of land surrounded by water on three sides.

Plains: a broad, nearly level area, often with low, gently rolling hills.

Plateaus: landforms that rise sharply above the level of surrounding land on at least one side. When a plateau rises sharply on all sides and has a flat top, it is called a *tableland*.

Valley: low land between mountains or hills.

IDENTIFYING LANDFORMS

1. With your pencil, trace the eastern and western *coastlines* of the *continent* of North America.
2. Circle the *capes* on the eastern coast of North America.
3. Identify all the *islands* on the map by placing a check mark on each one.
4. Place an X on the *isthmus* shown on the map.
5. Does the eastern or western part of North America have more *mountains?*

   _____

6. What symbol is used on the map to show mountains? _____ Why?

   _____

7. Locate the *peninsulas* on the map. Shade them or color them with your pencil.
8. Draw slanting lines over the part of North America where *plains* are probably located.
9. Study insets 3 and 4. How would you describe the difference between a *cape* and a *peninsula?* _____

   _____

10. Study insets 1 and 2. How would you describe the difference between a *valley* and *plains?* _____

    _____

8. Water Forms

Lesson 8 will show you how to:
• Recognize water forms on a map of North and Central America.

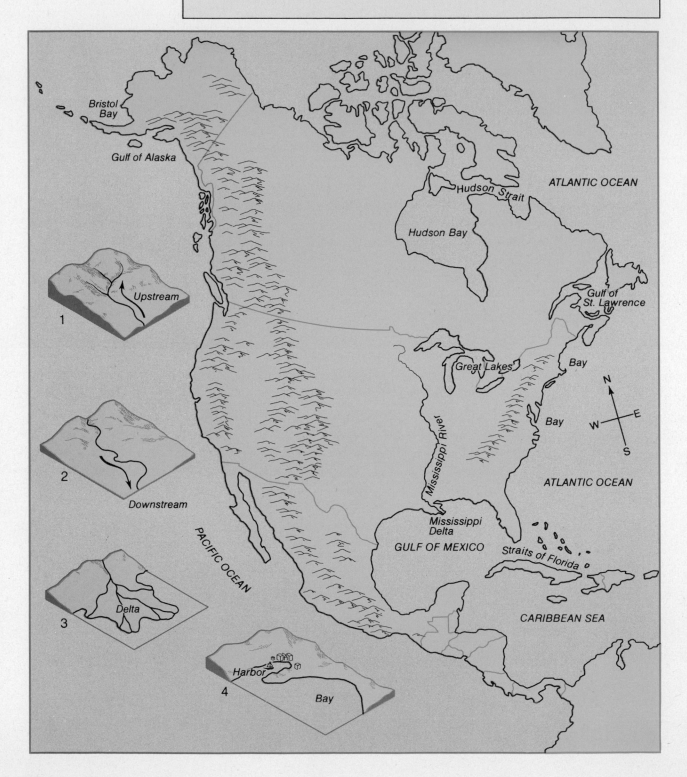

Bristol Bay

Gulf of Alaska

ATLANTIC OCEAN

Hudson Strait

Hudson Bay

Gulf of St. Lawrence

1 Upstream

Great Lakes

Bay

N

W E

S

2 Downstream

Bay

PACIFIC OCEAN

ATLANTIC OCEAN

3 Delta

Mississippi River

Mississippi Delta

GULF OF MEXICO

Straits of Florida

4 Harbor

Bay

CARIBBEAN SEA

24

The waters on the earth, as well as the lands, are shaped differently. *Water forms* are distinguished from each other by their size, their shape, and by the role they play in the life of other water forms.

For instance, we tell a lake by its shape. It is surrounded by land. We tell a bay by its shape—it is surrounded partly by land—and by its size—it is very large. And we tell a strait by the work it does. A strait connects two larger bodies of water.

Here is a list of the earth's most important water forms:

Bay: a part of an ocean protected by the land around it.

Delta: a wide, fan-shaped place located where a river empties into a larger body of water. A *delta* is made out of soil carried along by the river and deposited just before it joins the larger body of water. Several streams of water usually flow over a *delta.*

Downstream: the direction in which a river flows. Rivers always flow from high land to lower land. They can flow in any direction into a larger body of water. For example, the Nile River in Africa flows from south to north into the Mediterranean Sea.

Upstream: the direction from the end, or mouth, of a river to its source, or beginning. If you travel *upstream,* you are going against the flow of the river.

Source of a river: the place where a river begins. A river's *source* is in high land.

Mouth of a river: the place where a river empties into a larger body of water. A river's *mouth* is in low land.

Gulf: a body of water nearly surrounded by land. It is often larger than a bay, but not always so.

Harbor: a small- or medium-sized body of water protected by land.

Lake: a body of water completely surrounded by land.

Ocean: the largest body of water on the earth.

Sea: a large body of water either partly or completely surrounded by land. A *sea* can look like a gulf or a large lake.

Strait: a short, narrow passage of water that connects two larger bodies of water.

RECOGNIZING WATER FORMS

1. Locate the bays shown on the map and circle each one.

2. Find and circle the delta on the map. What body of water does it come from? _____

3. Locate the Mississippi River. With your pencil draw arrows showing the direction in which the river flows. Mark the source of the river with an S. Mark the mouth of the river with an M.

4. How many gulfs are shown on the map? _____

   How many are in the east? _____ How many are in

   the west? _____ How many are in the south?

   _____ How many are in the north? _____

   _____

5. How are these gulfs similar? _____

6. Is a gulf always larger than a bay? _____ Explain

   your answer. _____

7. Find the lakes on the map. Shade or color them with your pencil.

8. How does a lake differ from a bay? _____

   From a river? _____

9. Is the Atlantic Ocean east or west of North America? _____

10. How does the Caribbean Sea differ from the Gulf of Mexico? _____

    _____

11. What bodies of water are connected by the Hudson Strait and the Florida

    Straits? _____

12. Study insets 3 and 4. Describe the difference between a bay, a harbor, and

    a delta. _____

    _____

    _____

13. Study insets 1 and 2. Describe the difference between upstream and down-

    stream. _____

    _____

    _____

9. Land and Water Forms

Lesson 9 will show you how to:
• Identify each of the land and water forms shown on a map.

IDENTIFYING LAND AND WATER FORMS

Study the map. Then match the numbers of the land and water forms on the map with the names of land and water forms listed below it. Write the correct number in the spaces provided.

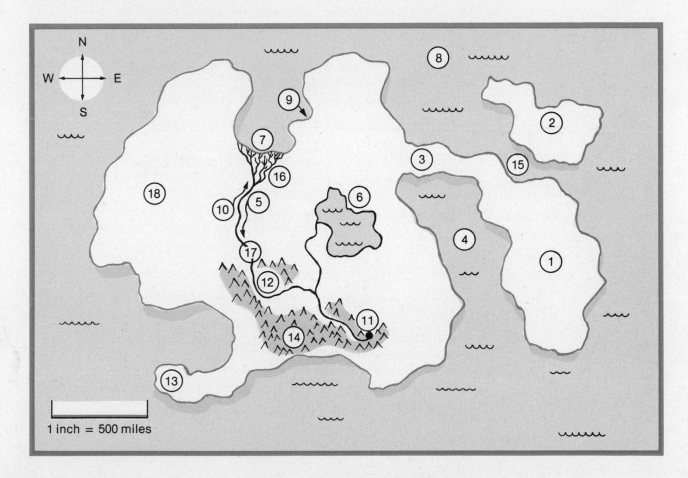

1 inch = 500 miles

1. _____ island	7. _____ river	13. _____ delta
2. _____ valley	8. _____ upstream	14. _____ downstream
3. _____ isthmus	9. _____ lake	15. _____ sea or ocean
4. _____ peninsula	10. _____ mountains	16. _____ source of a river
5. _____ harbor	11. _____ strait	17. _____ mouth of a river
6. _____ cape	12. _____ gulf or bay	18. _____ plains

27

10. Making a Map of a Continent

Lesson 10 will show you how to:
• Make a map of your own imaginary continent.

SHOW WHAT YOU KNOW

Up to this point, you have been reading maps made by others. Now you are ready to make your own map. Following the simple directions given below, draw a map of an imaginary continent on the next page.

A. In making your map of an imaginary continent, make sure you have a legend, or key, that includes:

   1. a scale of distance

   2. symbols for land and water forms

   3. symbols for anything else you want to show about your continent—for example, cities, forests, deserts, airports, highways, and so on

B. Show on your map at least one of the following:

   1. ocean or sea

   2. bay or gulf

   3. peninsula

   4. lake

   5. river

   6. cape

   7. mountains

C. Name each of the land and water forms you show on your map. Make sure the name will clearly identify each one—for example, Long Lake, High Mountains.

The Continent of

11. Making a Map of a State

> **Lesson 11 will show you how to:**
> • Make a map of your own imaginary state.

LET YOUR IMAGINATION GO

In Lesson 10, you drew a map of an imaginary continent. In this lesson, you will make a map of an imaginary state—a state you thought of yourself.

A. In making your map of an imaginary state, make sure you have a legend, or key, that includes:
   1. a scale of distance
   2. symbols for everything you want to show on the map
   3. a direction finder

B. On your map, show the following:
   1. a city or cities
   2. several towns
   3. roads and highways of different sizes
   4. a river or rivers
   5. an airport
   6. a lake or lakes
   7. a railroad
   8. a park or parks

C. Name the places and things on your map so they can be easily identified.

D. Make sure that your map gives a true picture of the things it shows; for example:
   1. Make sure rivers are shown flowing from high ground to low ground.
   2. If you show a bridge, be sure its purpose can easily be seen.
   3. Place cities and towns where you would expect them to be.
   4. Show clearly the source of a lake's water; for instance, show a river flowing into a lake.
   5. Make sure distances are real distances. For instance, on your scale of distance, one inch could equal 250 miles, but it should not equal 1 million miles or 5,000 miles.
   6. Make sure you place an airport where you would expect to find one—for example, near an area with many people.
   7. The border of your state should be drawn so that someone can tell whether it is bounded by other states or by water.

The State of

More Map Skills

12. Latitude

Lesson 12 will show you how to:
• Place points on the earth's surface by measuring latitude.

INTRODUCING LATITUDE

Take another look at the map of Post in Lesson 3. Notice how the streets and avenues form a grid pattern. Using the grid, we can describe the location of any place in Post. For example, the bank is on the northeast corner of Main Street and First Avenue North. The post office is on the northeast corner of Central Avenue and Main Street.

On many maps you will find a grid pattern that looks like the grid formed by Post's streets and avenues. The grid is formed by the crossing of lines of latitude and lines of longitude. Lines of latitude run in an east-west direction like the avenues of Post. Lines of longitude run in a north-south direction like Post's streets. In this lesson, you will learn how lines of latitude are used to place points on the earth's surface. You will learn about longitude in Lesson 14.

As you learned in Lesson 4, maps can show both visible and invisible things about the earth. Lines of latitude are among the invisible things that can be shown. They are imaginary lines on the earth's surface.

Remember how all the avenues in Post are identified as being so many blocks north or south of Central Avenue? Well, lines of latitude are identified in a similar way. The equator, the central line of latitude, is at zero *degrees* latitude. All the other lines of latitude are identified as being so many *degrees* north or south of the equator. For example, one line is called 15° north latitude; another is called 15° south latitude.

Lines of latitude are usually called *parallels*. This is because they are always the same distance apart, about 70 miles. No two lines of latitude ever meet.

Lines of latitude running around the earth look something like this:

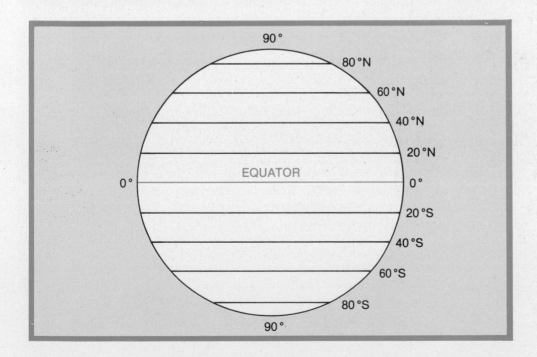

Beginning with zero degrees at the equator, we can measure up to ninety degrees north or south latitude. The North Pole is at 90° north latitude, and the South Pole is at 90° south latitude.

LOCATING PLACES WITH LATITUDE

A. The map below shows a large area on the earth such as a continent. Find place A. It is located 10° north of the equator, or 0°. We say it is 10° north latitude.

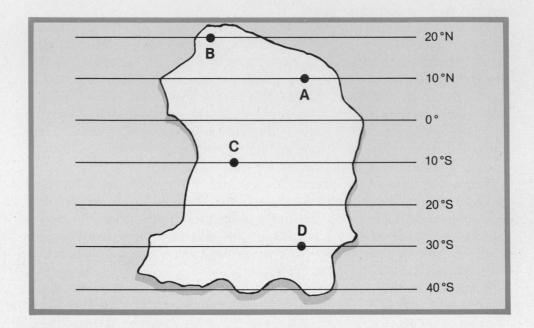

Write the locations of each of the following places in the space provided:

1. Place B _____

2. Place C _____

3. Place D _____

4. What do the locations of places A and C have in common? _____

_____

B. On maps of large areas on the earth, we usually do not find every parallel marked. On maps of smaller areas, however, we often find almost every parallel. The map below shows the island of Java. Write the location of each place in the space provided.

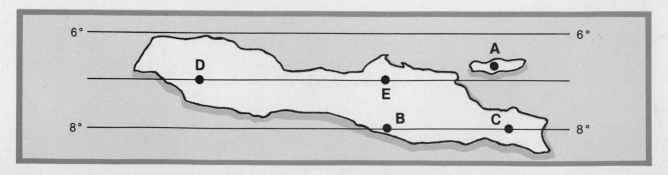

1. Place A is located at _____ latitude.

2. Place B is located at _____ latitude.

3. Place C is located at _____ latitude.

4. Place D is located at _____ latitude.

5. Place E is located at _____ latitude.

6. Which direction is the equator from the island of Java? _____

   How can you tell? _____

   _____

MORE PRACTICE FINDING LATITUDE

A. Use the map below to practice finding latitude. In the space provided, write the latitude of each place shown on the map.

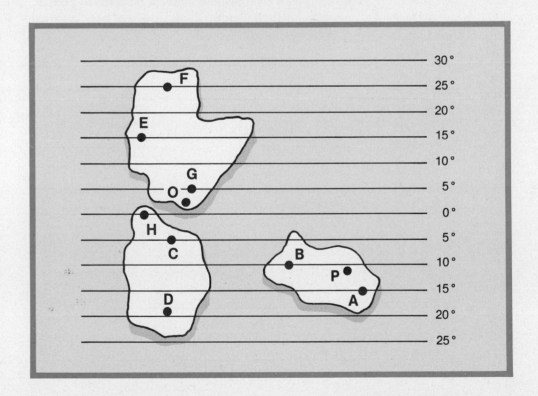

	Latitude	North or South		Latitude	North or South
1. A	_____	_____	6. F	_____	_____
2. B	_____	_____	7. G	_____	_____
3. C	_____	_____	8. H	_____	_____
4. D	_____	_____	9. O	_____	_____
5. E	_____	_____	10. P	_____	_____

13. Measuring Latitude

Lesson 13 will show you how to:
- Locate places by latitude on a map of Central America and South America.

PRACTICE MEASURING LATITUDE

A. Remember that maps of large areas usually do not show every line of latitude. So, many places on these maps will not be located on a parallel. We cannot tell the exact location of such places. Instead, we have to estimate their locations, using the parallels shown as guides. On the following map, for example:

1. Place C is not located on one of the parallels shown. It seems to be halfway between 0° and 10° north latitude. Therefore, we can say that Place C is located at about 5° north latitude.

2. Place D is not halfway between 0° and 10° south latitude. So, its location may be described as about 2° south latitude.

3. Place E is more than halfway between 10° and 20° south latitude. It is closer to 20° than to 10°. So, its location could be described as about 18° south latitude.

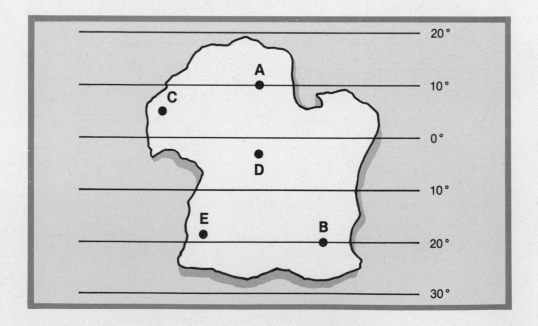

36

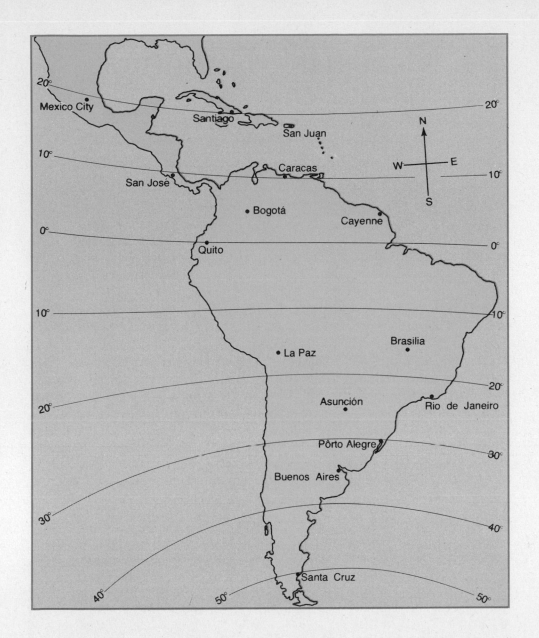

B. Study the map of Central and South America. Then give the latitude of each of the cities on the list.

City	Latitude	North or South	City	Latitude	North or South
Santa Cruz	_____	_____	Cayenne	_____	_____
Pôrto Alegre	_____	_____	Brasilia	_____	_____
Quito	_____	_____	Asunción	_____	_____
Buenos Aires	_____	_____	La Paz	_____	_____
Mexico City	_____	_____	Caracas	_____	_____
San José	_____	_____	Rio de Janeiro	_____	_____
Santiago	_____	_____	San Juan	_____	_____
Bogotá	_____	_____			

14. Measuring Longitude

Lesson 14 will show you how to:
• Place points on the earth's surface by measuring longitude.

INTRODUCING LONGITUDE

In Lessons 12 and 13, you learned that the latitude of any place on the earth is its distance north or south of the equator. Latitude helps us to locate places on the earth's surface. Parallels, lines of latitude, are like avenues in the town of Post.

However, we must know more than latitude to locate a place on the earth—just as we have to know more than the name of the avenue to locate a place in Post. Knowing that a family lives on Central Avenue is a help in finding their home. But, we can find it exactly if we know the house is at the place where Central Avenue meets 3rd Street East.

We locate places on the earth's surface in the same way. North-south imaginary lines on the earth are lines of *longitude*. They are called *meridians*. Just as we measured latitude from 0° (the equator), so, we measure longitude from 0°, the Prime Meridian or Main Meridian. The Prime Meridian, 0° longitude, passes through Greenwich, a suburb of London, England.

Meridians on the earth, then, are like the streets of Post. The streets of Post are identified as being so many blocks east or west of Main Street. Meridians are identified as being so many degrees east or west of the Prime Meridian.

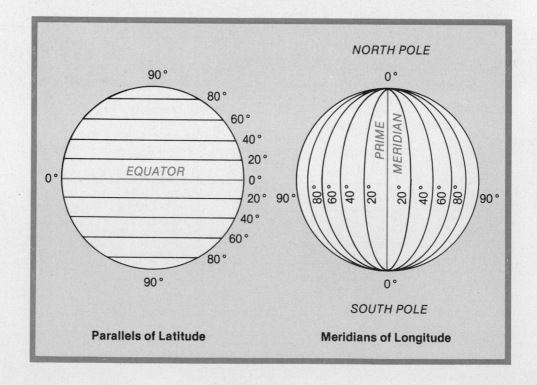

Parallels of Latitude   **Meridians of Longitude**

Meridians (lines of longitude) are not always the same distance apart. They meet at the North and South Poles. The nearer meridians are to the poles, the closer they are to each other. The diagram on page 38 shows the difference between parallels and meridians.

GLOBES, MAPS, AND LONGITUDE

A globe is the most accurate model of the earth. Like the earth, it is a sphere. On all globes, meridians of longitude are shown accurately. They are curved lines, and they meet at the poles.

Globes, however, are not always easy to use. Most globes are small and cannot show much about small areas on the earth. It is difficult to carry large globes from place to place. And, when we look at a globe, we can see only half the earth at one time. So, we use flat maps more frequently than globes.

A flat map is easy to carry around. It can show the whole world at one time. And, as you saw with the maps of Post, Lock, and Futura, a flat map can show a lot about small areas as well as big ones.

Flat maps, however, are not as accurate as globes. This is because a flat map does not have the same shape as the round earth. So, any time we picture the whole earth, or part of it, on a flat map, we must distort something—that is, we must show something inaccurately to show something else accurately.

For example, Map A below shows the meridians accurately as curved lines. It also shows the land areas of the earth in true relation to each other. But, unlike the earth, the map is flat at the poles and bulges at the sides. So, the shapes of land areas away from the center of the map are not accurate. Nor are the distances and directions correct.

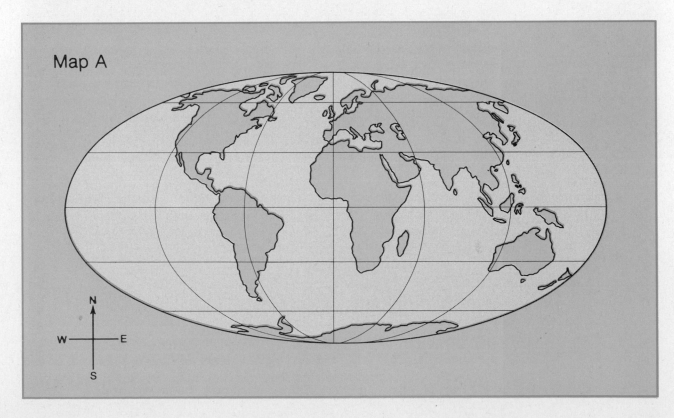

Map A

Map B below is the most commonly used map of the earth. It is called the Mercator map because it was first made by Gerhardus Mercator, an early Dutch mapmaker. Since his map was for sailors, Mercator wanted to show directions as accurately as possible. But in making directions correct, he could not make land sizes and distances correct, too. And he could not show meridians curving and meeting at the poles.

Therefore, on Mercator maps, the meridians are straight lines, and they do not meet at the poles. In addition, land and water areas are shown inaccurately, too. They are spread out, especially near the poles, and they are not shown in true size. As a result, distances near the edges of the map are not accurate.

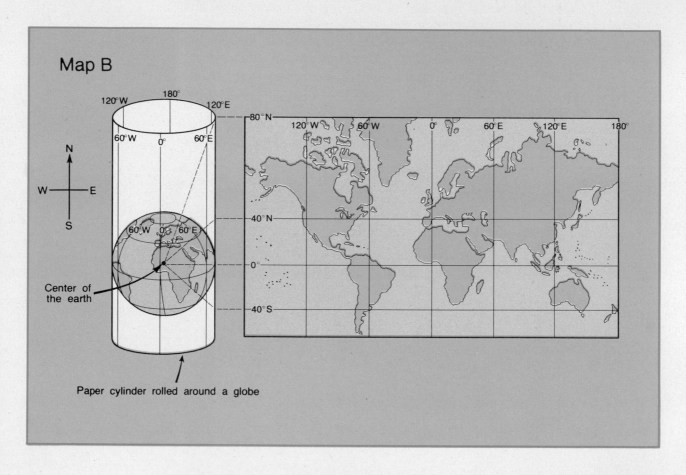

Compare the Mercator map, shown above right, with the globe, shown above left. A paper cylinder is shown rolled around the globe in order to give you some idea of just how much the map distorts information about the earth.

PRACTICE MEASURING LONGITUDE

A. Locate, by giving longitude, each of the places shown on this map of forty-eight of the fifty United States. Notice that some places are not located exactly on one of the meridians shown on the map. For these places, you have to estimate the degree of longitude.

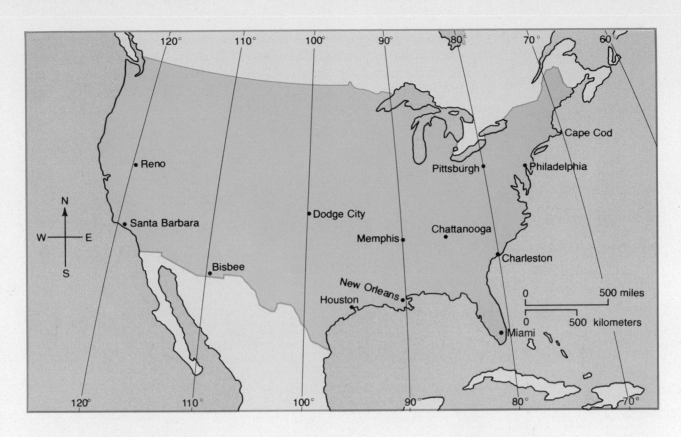

1. Dodge City, Kansas _____

2. Bisbee, New Mexico _____

3. New Orleans, Louisiana _____

4. Miami, Florida _____

5. Charleston, South Carolina _____

6. Cape Cod, Massachusetts _____

7. Pittsburgh, Pennsylvania _____

8. Reno, Nevada _____

9. Memphis, Tennessee _____

10. Santa Barbara, California _____

11. Philadelphia, Pennsylvania _____

12. Chattanooga, Tennessee _____

13. Houston, Texas _____

14. Is the United States located east or west of the Prime Meridian?

_____

15. If you lived in Philadelphia, would the Prime Meridian be east or west

of you? _____

B. Now you are going to look at meridians on a map of a smaller area, the state of Alaska and the northwest part of Canada. Once again, locate the places on the map by giving their longitude. Remember that some places are not located exactly on one of the meridians shown on the map. You must estimate the location of these places.

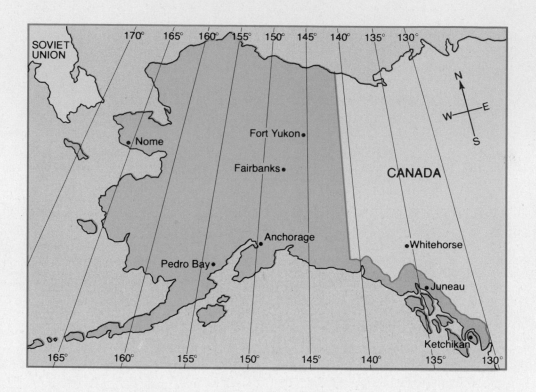

1. Nome _____

2. Pedro Bay _____

3. Anchorage _____

4. Fort Yukon _____

5. Whitehorse, Canada _____

6. Juneau _____

7. Ketchikan _____

8. Fairbanks _____

15. Measuring Latitude and Longitude

Lesson 15 will show you how to:
- Use latitude and longitude to locate places on the earth *exactly*.
- Compare the information about latitude and longitude given on two different maps.

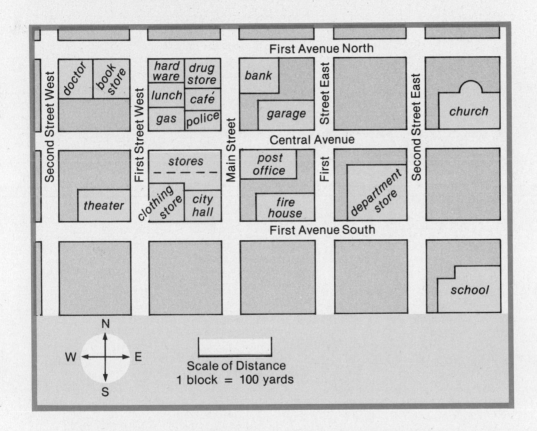

Remember the map of Post in Lesson 3? Take a moment now to study a section of it again. As you see, we can describe the location of places in Post in three different ways. We can say, for instance, that the department store is located on Second Street East. We can say that it is located on First Avenue South. Or, we can say that it is located at the point where the two cross—on the corner of Second Street East and First Avenue South.

Using latitude and longitude, we can locate places on the earth in similar ways. For example, we can describe the location of Cairo, Egypt, as 32° north latitude. We can describe it as 30° east longitude. Or, we can give both latitude and longitude, saying that Cairo is located at 32° north latitude and 30° east longitude. By giving both latitude and longitude, we can pinpoint the location of Cairo exactly.

LOCATING CITIES IN THE UNITED STATES AND CANADA

Study the map of the United States and Canada. Then answer the questions. Remember to give *both* latitude and longitude when they are asked for.

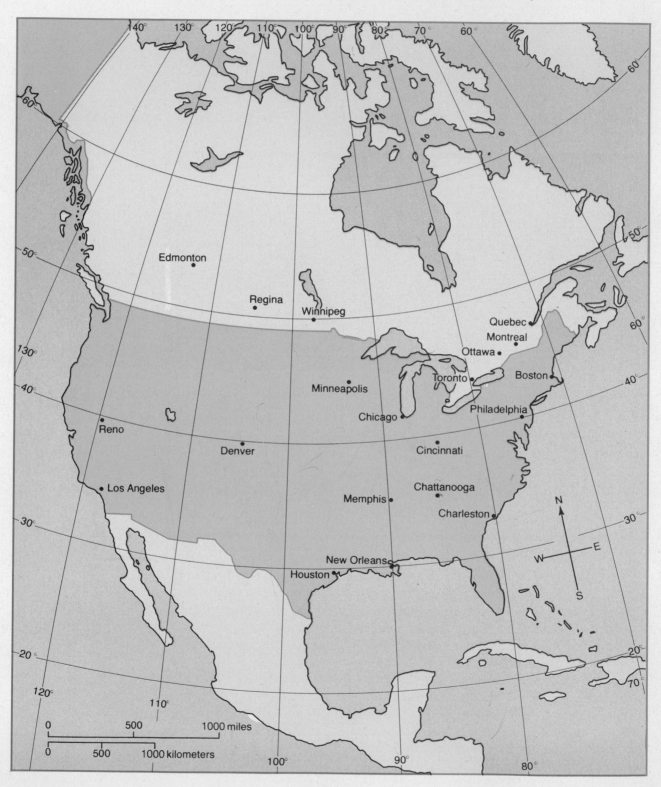

A. Identify the city located at each of the following places:

1. 90° W long., 30° N lat. _____

2. 105° W long., 40° N lat. _____

3. 113° W long., 54° N lat. _____

4. 95° W long., 30° N lat. _____

5. 85° W long., 35° N lat. _____

6. 85° W long., 39° N lat. _____

7. 105° W long., 50° N lat. _____

B. Give the latitude and longitude of the following cities:

1. Los Angeles, California _____° _____ long., _____° _____ lat.

2. Chicago, Illinois _____° _____ long., _____° _____ lat.

3. Reno, Nevada _____° _____ long., _____° _____ lat.

4. Montreal, Canada _____° _____ long., _____° _____ lat.

5. Boston, Massachusetts _____° _____ long., _____° _____ lat.

6. Minneapolis, Minnesota _____° _____ long., _____° _____ lat.

7. Winnipeg, Canada _____° _____ long., _____° _____ lat.

8. Charleston,
   South Carolina _____° _____ long., _____° _____ lat.

C. 1. In which direction is the Prime Meridian from the United States?

   _____

   2. In which direction is the equator from the United States?

   _____

D. Which city is farther *east*?

1. New Orleans or Chattanooga? _____

2. Chicago or Minneapolis? _____

3. Montreal or Boston _____

4. Reno or Los Angeles? _____

E. Which city is farther *north*?

1. Denver or Chicago? _____

2. Montreal or Chicago? _____

3. Philadelphia or Cincinnati? _____

4. Charleston or Houston? _____

LOCATING CITIES IN EUROPE

Study the map of Europe. Then answer the questions that follow. Remember to give *both* latitude and longitude when they are asked for.

A. Give the location of each of the following places:

1. Oslo, Norway   _____° _____ long., _____° _____ lat.

2. Helsinki, Finland   _____° _____ long., _____° _____ lat.

3. Prague, Czechoslovakia   _____° _____ long., _____° _____ lat.

4. Toledo, Spain   _____° _____ long., _____° _____ lat.

5. Belgrade, Yugoslavia   _____° _____ long., _____° _____ lat.

6. London, England   _____° _____ long., _____° _____ lat.

7. Leningrad, Soviet Union   _____° _____ long., _____° _____ lat.

8. Hamburg, Germany   _____° _____ long., _____° _____ lat.

B. Which place is located at each of the following points?

1. 6° W long., 55° N lat. _____

2. 33° E long., 40° N lat. _____

3. 15° E long., 42° N lat. _____

4. 22° W long., 64° N lat. _____

5. 0° long., 48° N lat. _____

6. 38° E long., 56° N lat. _____

7. 25° E long., 35° N lat. _____

8. 5° E long., 52° N lat. _____

COMPARING INFORMATION ON TWO MAPS

Using the map of Europe and the map of the United States, tell whether each of these statements is true (T) or false (F).

_____ 1. Winnipeg, Canada, is farther from the equator than Moscow, Soviet Union.

_____ 2. Toledo, Spain, and Philadelphia, Pennsylvania, are the same distance from the equator.

_____ 3. An airplane flying from Chicago to London would travel southeast.

_____ 4. All of Europe is farther from the equator than New Orleans.

_____ 5. No line of longitude in Europe is the same as a line of longitude in the United States.

16. Using a Variety of Maps

LEARNING TO READ DIFFERENT KINDS OF MAPS

There is almost no limit to the kinds of maps we use today or to the kinds of information we can show on maps. Every year mapmakers find new ways to picture things on the earth and about the earth.

Certain maps, however, are used more often than others. The three most commonly used maps are political maps, physical maps, and population maps.

A. Political Maps

Political maps show us the location and boundaries of governmental units, large and small. For example, a political map of the whole world will show the different nations of the world. A political map of one nation will usually show the nation's states or provinces. And the political map of a state will show the boundaries of counties, cities, towns, and villages.

On most political maps of large areas, you will find the capital city and the other important cities of the area. To find out what a political map shows, be sure to look at the map's legend or key.

A political map of part of the United States appears on the next page. Study the key to find out what each symbol means. Then answer the questions that follow.

1. What is the capital of Ohio? _____

   How can you tell? _____

   _____

2. What is the capital of Illinois? _____

3. Is Pittsburgh the capital of Pennsylvania? _____

   How can you tell? _____

   _____

4. Is St. Louis the capital of Missouri? _____

5. How many states does Kentucky border? _____

6. How many states does Indiana border? _____

7. Without looking at the map or at the questions you have just answered,

complete this statement: A political map shows _____

_____

_____

_____

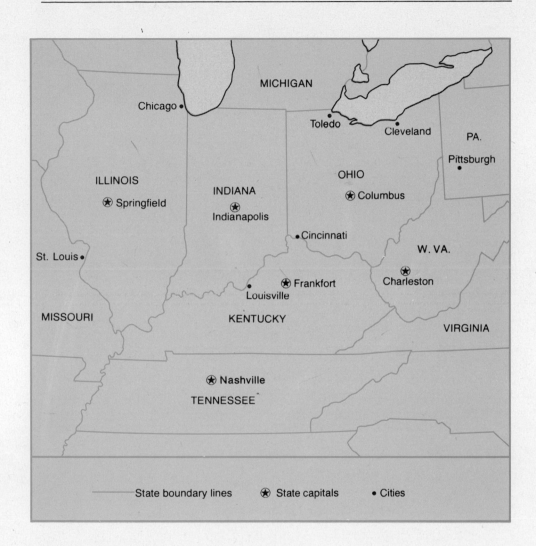

MICHIGAN

Chicago •

Toledo •
Cleveland •

PA.

Pittsburgh •

ILLINOIS
INDIANA
OHIO

⊛ Springfield
⊛
Indianapolis
⊛ Columbus

• Cincinnati

W. VA.

St. Louis •

⊛ Frankfort
• Louisville
⊛
Charleston

MISSOURI
KENTUCKY

VIRGINIA

⊛ Nashville
TENNESSEE

—— State boundary lines   ⊛ State capitals   • Cities

B. *Physical Maps*

Physical maps show plains, plateaus, hills, mountains, lakes, deserts, forests, and other important physical features of a part of the earth. Usually physical maps show these features in colors.

The same colors are often used to show the same things on many different physical maps. For example, nearly all physical maps use blue to show bodies of water. Many use green to show forested places and browns and yellows to show places that are high or dry or both.

Physical maps use other symbols, too. The legend on the physical map of the United States which follows shows some of these symbols. Study the map. Then answer the questions.

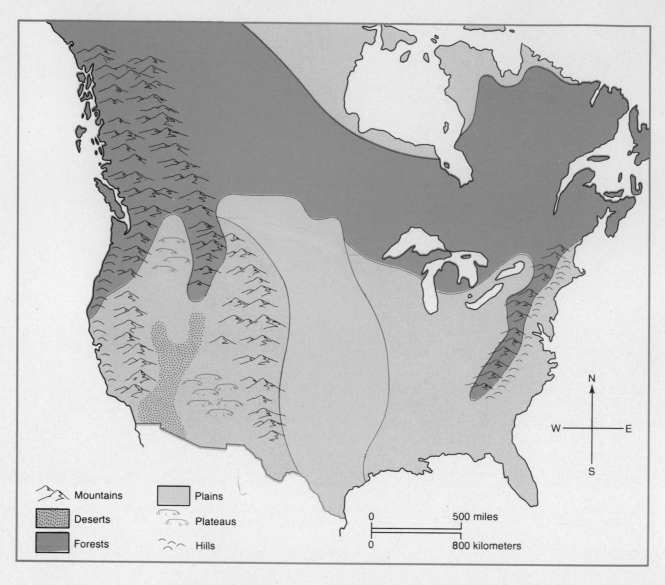

Legend:
- Mountains
- Deserts
- Forests
- Plains
- Plateaus
- Hills

0 ——— 500 miles
0 ——— 800 kilometers

1. What symbol is used on the map to show the mountains? _____

2. What part of the United States is most mountainous? _____

3. What symbol is used on the map to show plains? _____

4. Describe the location of the plains areas of Canada. _____
   _____
   _____
   _____

5. How many plateau areas are found in the United States? _____
   Where are they located? _____

6. What symbol is used on the map to show forests? _____

7. If you were traveling in the United States from the plateaus to the plains, in what direction would you go? _____

17. Comparing Information on Three Kinds of Maps

Lesson 17 will show you how to:
- Read three different kinds of maps.
- Put together information from three different maps to draw conclusions about places on the earth.

POPULATION MAPS

Population maps show *where* people live on the earth and *how many* people live on the earth or parts of it. With population maps we can see where on the earth people are crowded together and where they have a lot of space.

Population maps do not tell us *why* people live in certain areas. Instead, they tell us about the *population density* of an area. In other words, they tell us how many people occupy every square foot, or square acre, or square mile of the earth.

Density comes from the word *dense* which means thick or crowded.

For example, suppose two classrooms in your school are exactly the same size. Classroom A has forty students and Classroom B has twenty. It is easy to see that Classroom A is more crowded than Classroom B. We can say that Classroom A has a *higher population density* than Classroom B because more people take up the same space.

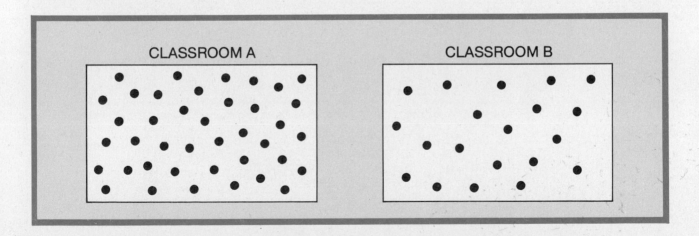

When we talk about population density, we usually speak of the *average* number of people who occupy a space. Let's take the two classrooms as an example. Suppose both Classroom A and Classroom B take up four hundred square feet of space. The *average population density* of Classroom A is one pupil for every ten square feet and that of Classroom B is one pupil for every twenty square feet.

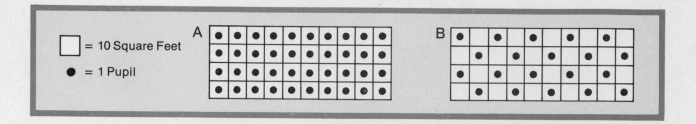

= 10 Square Feet

● = 1 Pupil

A

B

Of course, this is not an exact picture of how space is used in the class-rooms. Classroom A might have desks spaced evenly around the room. And Classroom B might have all the desks crowded into one corner, leaving the rest of the space open. We use averages to give a general picture of the population density of a space. We don't use them to show how space is occupied in detail.

WHERE PEOPLE LIVE IN THE UNITED STATES

Here is a map of the United States. The states of Alaska and Hawaii are insets. Study the map to find out where people in the United States live. Then tell whether each of the following statements is true (T) or false (F). Write an N in the space if you cannot tell from the map whether the statement is true or false.

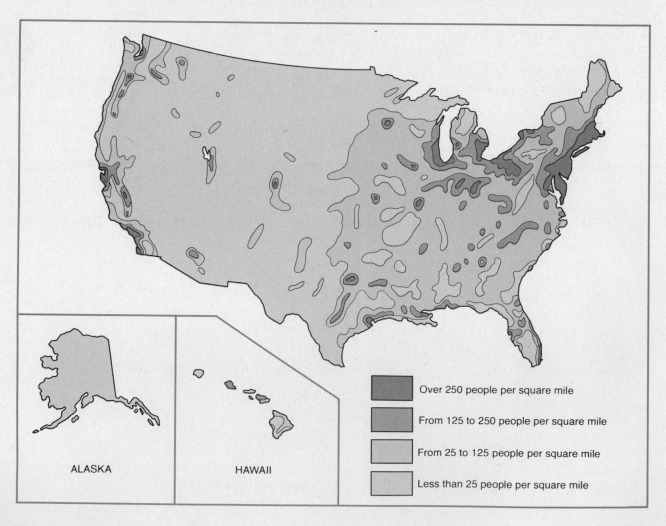

ALASKA

HAWAII

Over 250 people per square mile

From 125 to 250 people per square mile

From 25 to 125 people per square mile

Less than 25 people per square mile

_____ 1. The *Northeast* is the most densely populated part of the United States.

_____ 2. In almost half the United States, there are fewer than 25 people for each square mile of land.

_____ 3. There are no places in southern United States where there are 250 people per square mile of land.

_____ 4. Sometimes there is a densely populated place in the middle of an area with a few people.

_____ 5. Most people live in the parts of the country with the heaviest rainfall.

_____ 6. The state of Alaska has between 25 and 125 people for every square mile of land.

_____ 7. Each of the islands of Hawaii is among the most crowded parts of the United States.

_____ 8. The most densely populated parts of the western United States are along the seacoast.

_____ 9. In the eastern half of the United States, the places with the fewest people are mountainous.

_____ 10. Surrounding the areas of great population density in the West are areas where there are 125 to 250 people for every square mile.

RAINFALL MAPS

A rainfall map shows the average amount of rain that falls in an area in a certain period of time. The amount of rain is shown in inches. Usually the map shows rainfall for a whole year. However, rainfall maps can show the amount of rain that falls over shorter periods of time.

A. The rainfall map on page 54 shows how much rain falls in each part of the United States in a normal year. Study the map, especially the legend. Then tell whether the statements that follow are true (T) or false (F). The italicized words make the statement true or false. What word or words would you substitute to make the false statement true?

_____ 1. Some parts of the western United States receive *less than ten inches* of rain in a normal year.

_____ 2. Almost all of the eastern part of the United States receives *sixty or more* inches of rain in a normal year.

_____ 3. Parts of the Northwest receive *eighty or more* inches of rain in a normal year.

_____ 4. *Alaska and Hawaii* receive some of the heaviest rainfall in the entire country.

_____ 5. The driest parts of the country are found in the *Southeast.*

_____ 6. If you wanted to live in an area that receives sixty to eighty inches of rain a year, you would have to live in the *center of* the United States.

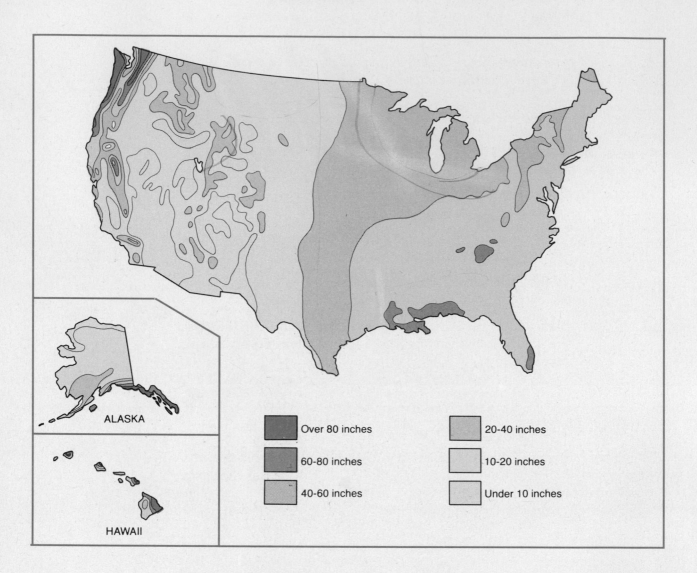

ALASKA

HAWAII

Over 80 inches	20-40 inches
60-80 inches	10-20 inches
40-60 inches	Under 10 inches

B. We now have information about the *average population density* and the *average rainfall* of the United States. We can use both maps together to gain additional information. Study the maps again. Then tell whether these statements are true (T) or false (F).

_____ 1. The eastern half of the United States has the greatest density of population. But its rainfall is neither heavy nor light.

_____ 2. Places in Alaska and Hawaii with the heaviest rainfall also have the greatest density of population.

_____ 3. Wherever there are 250 people per square mile along the northeast coast of the United States, rainfall is from forty to sixty inches per year.

_____ 4. In general, the areas of the United States with the heaviest rainfall are not the most densely populated.

_____ 5. People seem to want to live in places with the heaviest rainfall.

_____ 6. Large areas with little rainfall also have the fewest people per
square mile of land.

MAPPING FARM PRODUCTS

We will look now at another kind of map, a *product map*. This map shows
the farm products of the United States. The products are shown in the general
area in which they are produced in large amounts. Study the map. Then tell
whether each of the statements that follow is true (T) or false (F).

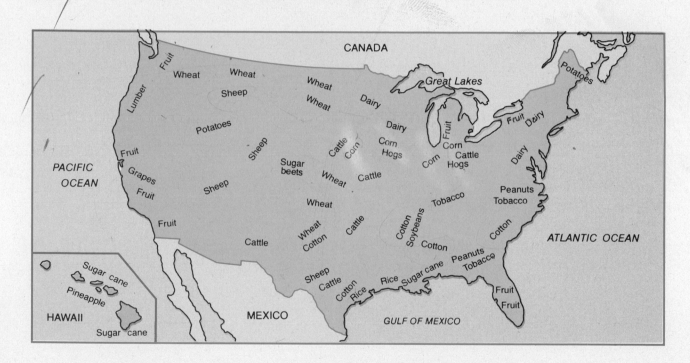

_____ 1. Rice and sugar cane are products of the southern part of the
United States near the Gulf of Mexico.

_____ 2. Fruits seem to be grown far from large bodies of water.

_____ 3. Tobacco is a product of southeastern United States.

_____ 4. Corn is an important farm product in almost every part of the
United States.

_____ 5. Hogs and sheep are usually raised in the same places.

_____ 6. Important dairy regions are located in the central part of the
country.

_____ 7. Cotton is a product of the southern and southeastern states.

COMBINING INFORMATION ON THREE MAPS

You are now ready to use all three maps together—the population map, the rainfall map, and the product map. Read each of the following statements carefully. Study the maps to find out if the statements are correct. Then place a T (true) or an F (false) in the space before each statement.

_____ 1. Sheep and cattle are usually raised in areas that are not densely populated.

_____ 2. Wheat appears to be a product that can be raised in drier parts of the country.

_____ 3. Rice and sugar cane are raised in areas where there will be more than sixty inches of rain.

_____ 4. The cotton areas of the United States are those with ten to twenty inches of rainfall.

_____ 5. Sheep raising and little rainfall seem to go together.

_____ 6. Corn and hogs are important farm products in areas where there are fewer than 25 people per square mile of land.

_____ 7. Dairy products, heavy population, and good rainfall seem to go together.

18. More Practice with Population, Rainfall, and Product Maps

Lesson 18 will show you how to:
- Practice reading three different kinds of maps.
- Put together information from several maps.
- Draw conclusions from the information on several maps.

In Lesson 17 you learned how to read three different kinds of maps: population maps, rainfall maps, and product maps. You also discovered how to draw conclusions about a place by combining and comparing the information on several different maps.

The skills you learned in Lesson 17 can be used in learning more about any country or region of the world. In this lesson you will use these skills to gather information about the continent of Africa.

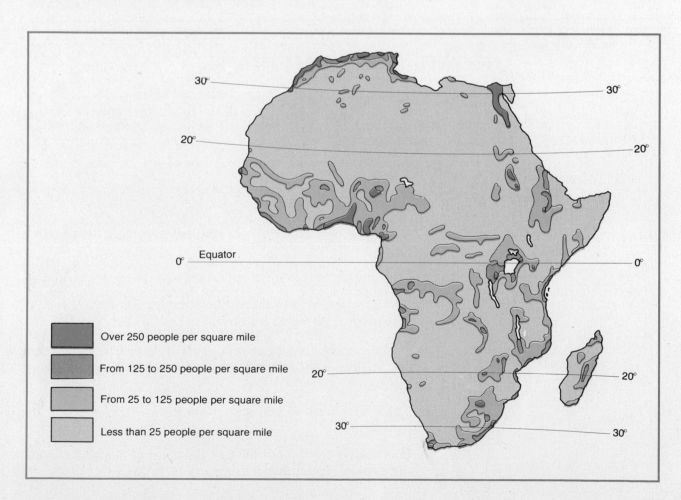

- Over 250 people per square mile
- From 125 to 250 people per square mile
- From 25 to 125 people per square mile
- Less than 25 people per square mile

WHERE PEOPLE LIVE IN AFRICA

On the preceding page is a population map of Africa. Study the map carefully, especially the legend. Then place a check before each correct statement.

_____ 1. Most of the areas with more than 250 people per square mile are in the center of the African continent.

_____ 2. There are several places along the seacoast of Africa where there are more than 250 people per square mile.

_____ 3. Most of Africa has fewer than 25 people per square mile.

_____ 4. The most heavily populated part of Africa is along the western coast.

_____ 5. The first impression you get from the map is that there are very few people in most parts of Africa.

_____ 6. In the parts of Africa with the warmest weather, there are no places with a dense population.

_____ 7. At 20° north latitude or south latitude, there are no areas of heavy population.

THE AVERAGE RAINFALL IN AFRICA

A. The map on page 59 shows the average yearly rainfall of Africa. Study the map carefully. Then tell whether each of the following statements is true (T) or false (F). Write a T or F in the space provided. The italicized words make a statement true or false. If the statement is false, cross out the italicized words and substitute the correct word or words to make it true.

_____ 1. Around the equator, there are large areas where rainfall is *more than sixty inches a year.*

_____ 2. Almost all of northern Africa receives *twenty inches* of rain a year.

_____ 3. The *central* part of Africa appears to receive the most rainfall.

_____ 4. Along the seacoasts in the southwestern part of Africa, rainfall is *more than 40 inches a year.*

_____ 5. Because of the amount of rain that falls on northern, eastern, and southwestern areas of Africa, these places can be called *deserts.*

_____ 6. The largest areas of very heavy rainfall in Africa are near the *equator.*

_____ 7. Immediately north and south of the areas of heaviest rainfall, the average rainfall is *ten to twenty inches* a year.

COMPARING INFORMATION ON TWO MAPS

A. Study the map of rainfall here and the rainfall map in Lesson 17. Then compare the average yearly rainfall of Africa with that of the United States. Place a check before the statements that are correct. (Remember that the continent of Africa is more than twice the size of the United States.)

_____ 1. Africa has larger areas in which more than sixty inches of rain falls each year than does the United States.

_____ 2. Both Africa and the United States have large areas in which little rain falls each year.

_____ 3. The entire eastern coast of the United States receives a great deal of rainfall, while Africa has some extremely dry areas along its eastern coast.

_____ 4. The heaviest rainfall is in the center of both Africa and the United States.

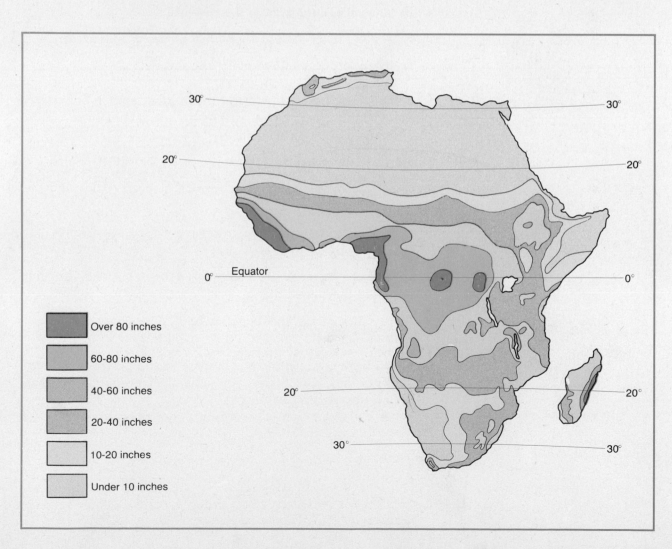

▨	Over 80 inches
▨	60-80 inches
▨	40-60 inches
▨	20-40 inches
▨	10-20 inches
▨	Under 10 inches

THE FARM PRODUCTS OF AFRICA

A. The map to the right shows the farm products of Africa. Study it carefully. Then combine the information on this map with the map of African rainfall to tell whether the following statements are true (T) or false (F). The italicized words make each statement true or false. If the statement is false, cross out the italicized words and substitute the correct word or words to make it true.

_____ 1. Cocoa, palm oil, and rubber are products of the *wettest* parts of Africa.

_____ 2. Sheep and goats are animals raised in areas *of little rainfall.*

_____ 3. In Africa, wheat is grown where rainfall is *more than sixty* inches a year.

_____ 4. Camels are animals of the *desert.*

_____ 5. Cotton is raised in Africa where there is at *least forty inches of rain* a year.

_____ 6. Bananas need *little rainfall* to grow well.

_____ 7. Olives and dates need at *least forty inches of rain* a year.

_____ 8. Fruits are products raised *along the seacoast.*

B. Study the map of farm products here and the product map in Lesson 17. Then compare the farm products of Africa with those of the United States. Place a check before the correct statements.

_____ 1. Africa has many products not grown in the United States.

_____ 2. Sheep are raised in the drier regions of both Africa and the United States.

_____ 3. Wheat, tobacco, and grapes are grown in the United States, but they cannot be grown in Africa.

_____ 4. Cocoa and bananas are grown in Africa, but they are not grown in the United States.

_____ 5. Large dairy farms are found in both Africa and the United States.

_____ 6. If you were a farmer living along the western or northwestern coasts of the United States, you would feel most at home along the northwest coast of Africa.

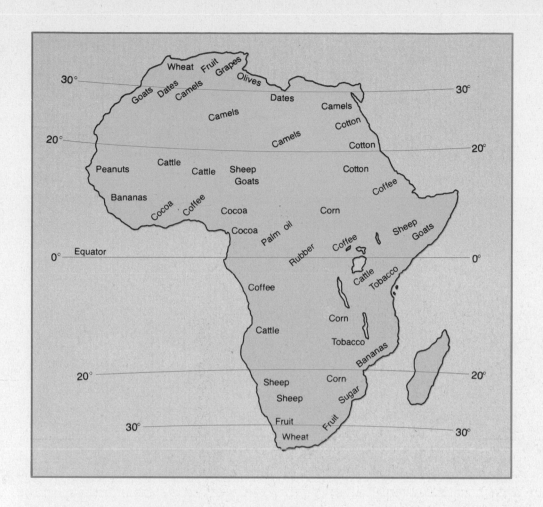

UNIT 3
Graph Skills

19. Introducing Graphs

Lesson 19 will show you how to:
- Recognize a graph—that is, a kind of chart that shows how two or more ideas are related.
- Read a picture graph.

WHAT IS A GRAPH?

1 gallon of lemonade

A graph is a kind of chart. Graphs show how two or more ideas are related. Often, graphs can show relationship more clearly than words can.

There are many different kinds of graphs—circle graphs, bar graphs, line graphs, and picture graphs. Each uses a different method to show how ideas are related. In this lesson we will study picture graphs, or *pictographs.*

A *pictograph* uses pictures to stand for the things to be related and compared. For example, a small picture of a glass could be used to stand for one gallon of lemonade. Two pictures of the glass would stand for two gallons, etc.

The pictures, or symbols, used on a pictograph do not always stand for only one thing, however. One symbol—the glass, for instance—could stand for one gallon, for two gallons, for ten gallons, for even ten thousand gallons. Like maps, graphs use keys, or legends, to tell what each symbol means. So, always be sure to check the key before you begin to read the graph.

A. The following graph shows how much lemonade Larry sold at his stand on a public golf course in one week. As you can see, each symbol represents one gallon of lemonade. Study the graph. Then answer the questions.

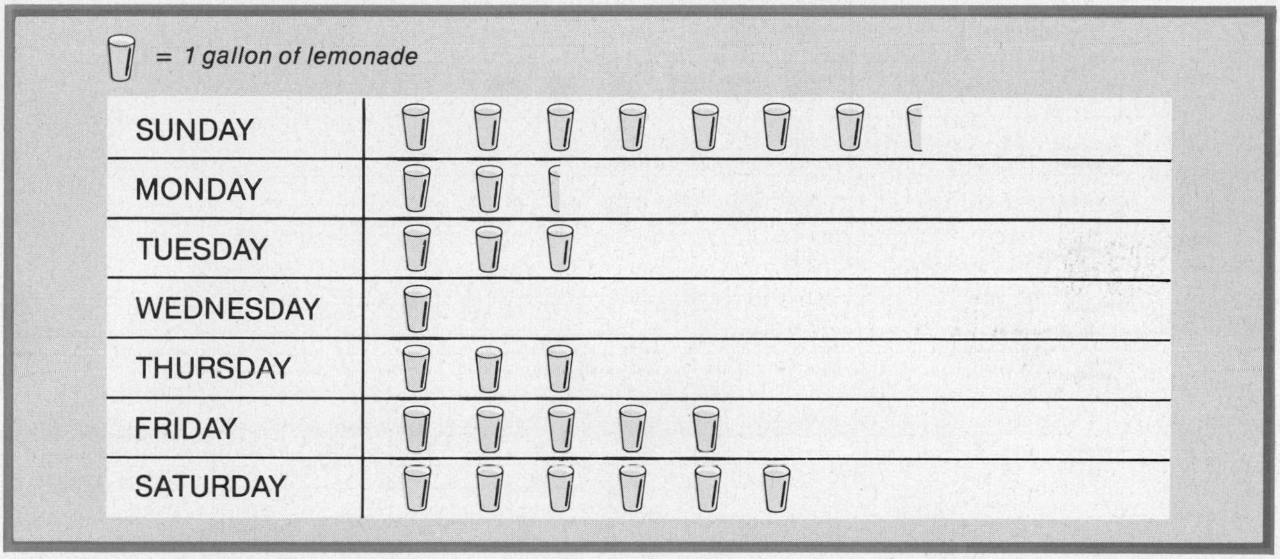

= 1 gallon of lemonade

SUNDAY	🥛 🥛 🥛 🥛 🥛 🥛 🥛 🥛
MONDAY	🥛 🥛 🥛
TUESDAY	🥛 🥛 🥛
WEDNESDAY	🥛
THURSDAY	🥛 🥛 🥛
FRIDAY	🥛 🥛 🥛 🥛 🥛
SATURDAY	🥛 🥛 🥛 🥛 🥛 🥛

1. On what day of the week did Larry sell the fewest gallons of lemonade? _____ How much did he sell on this day?

_____

2. On which days of the week did Larry sell the most lemonade? _____

_____

How much did he sell on each of these days? _____

_____

3. On which days did Larry sell the same amount of lemonade? _____

_____ How much lemonade did he

sell on these days? _____

4. If you were Larry's boss, how could this graph help you run your

lemonade business? _____

_____

B. This graph shows how long it takes the average Canadian worker to earn enough money to buy such things as bread, milk, butter, juice, and the daily newspaper. Study the graph. Then answer the questions that follow. Be sure to check the legend to see what the symbols stand for.

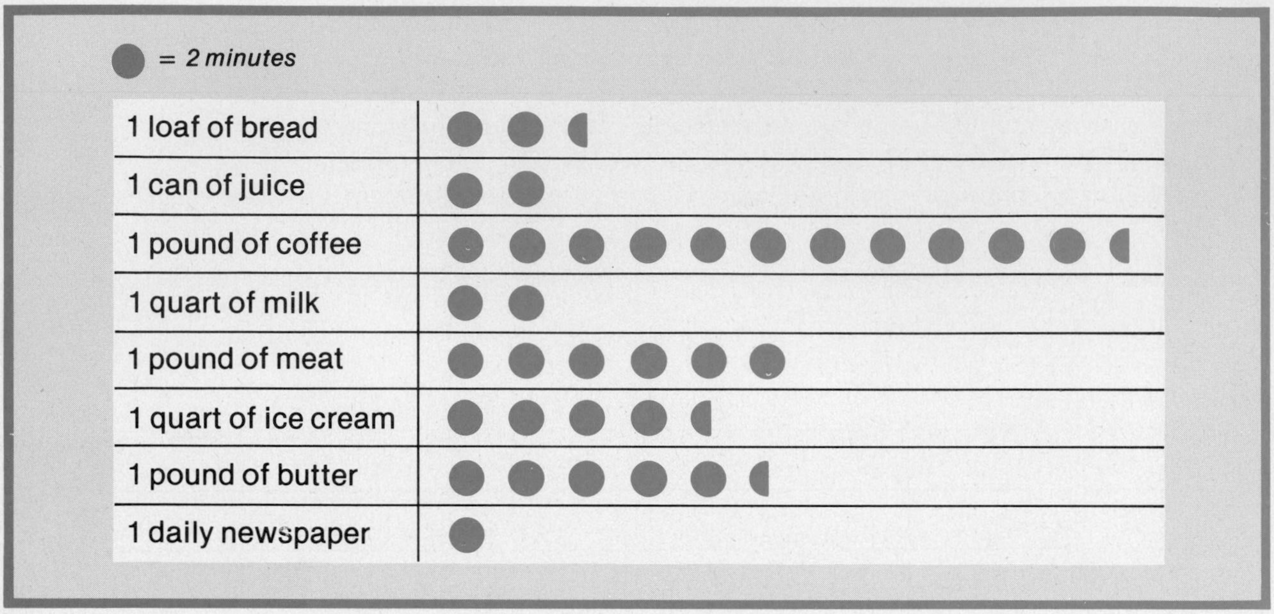

● = 2 minutes

1 loaf of bread	● ● ◖
1 can of juice	● ●
1 pound of coffee	● ● ● ● ● ● ● ● ● ● ◖
1 quart of milk	● ●
1 pound of meat	● ● ● ● ●
1 quart of ice cream	● ● ● ◖
1 pound of butter	● ● ● ● ◖
1 daily newspaper	●

. 1. How many minutes does it take the average worker to earn enough to buy one can of juice? _____ one quart of milk? _____ one pound of meat? _____ _____ one quart of ice cream? _____ one loaf of bread? _____ one pound of coffee? _____ two daily newspapers? _____ _____ two pounds of butter? _____

2. Does it take longer to earn enough to buy a pound of butter or a pound of meat? _____

3. Could a worker earn enough in ten minutes to buy a loaf of bread and a quart of milk? _____

4. Could a worker earn enough in a half hour to buy a pound of coffee and a pound of butter? _____

C. The following graph shows how many people came to the United States in 1975 and where they came from. As you can see, each symbol stands for ten thousand people. Study the graph carefully. Then tell whether each of the following statements is true (T) or false (F). Write an N in the space if you cannot tell from the information on the graph whether the statement is true or false.

☻ = 10,000 people		
MEXICO	☻☻☻☻☻☻☻	
PHILIPPINES	☻☻☻	
KOREA	☻☻☻	
WEST INDIES	☻☻☻☻☻☻	
TAIWAN	☻⌇	
ITALY	☻⌇	
GREECE	☻	
GERMANY	⌇	

_____ 1. In 1975, 10,000 people came from Greece to the United States.

_____ 2. In 1975, 70,000 people came from Mexico to the United States.

_____ 3. In 1975, more people came from Mexico to the United States than from any other country.

_____ 4. About 25,000 people came from Italy to the United States in 1975.

_____ 5. If they are added together, the number of people who came from the Philippines and Korea to the United States in 1975 equals the number of people who came from Mexico.

_____ 6. Most of the people who came to the United States from Mexico in 1975 came to find better-paying jobs.

_____ 7. Fewer than 10,000 people came to the United States from Germany in 1975.

_____ 8. More people came to the United States from the West Indies in 1975 than from Italy, Greece, and Germany combined.

9. Mexico and the West Indies are located in the region we call Latin America. The Philippines and Korea are in Asia. Italy, Greece, and Germany are in Europe. Using this information and the information on the graph, what general statements can we make about the people who came to the United States in 1975?

_____

_____

_____

20. Working with Bar Graphs

> **Lesson 20 will show you how to:**
> - Read a graph in which bars stand for the things to be related.
> - Recognize the kinds of ideas that can be pictured on a bar graph.

READING SIMPLE BAR GRAPHS

Usually, information that can be shown on a pictograph can also be shown on a bar graph. For example, the following graph uses bars to show much of the same information that was shown on the pictograph in Lesson 19.

A. Study the bar graph for a few minutes. Notice that the numbered lines show the minutes someone would have to work to earn enough to buy each of the items in the column on the left. Jot down the number of minutes for each item. Then compare your results with the answers to exercise B in Lesson 19.

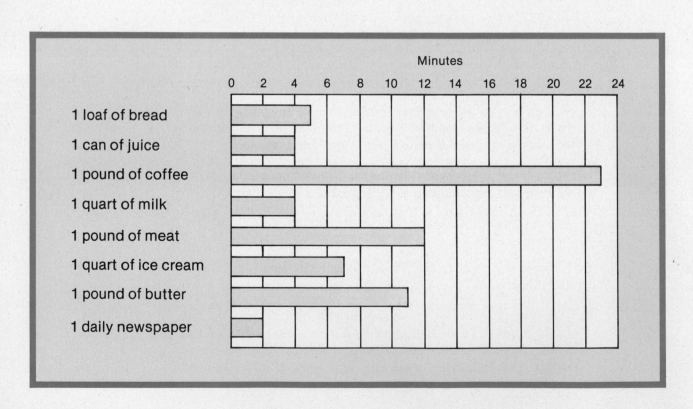

1. Are there any differences between the information given on the bar graph and the information given on the pictograph? _____

2. Which graph was easier for you to use? _____

   Why? _____

   _____

   _____

B. This bar graph shows how many millions of barrels of oil were produced in 1976 by the nations listed in the left-hand column. Study the graph. Then tell whether each of the following statements is true (T) or false (F). Write an N in the space if you cannot tell from the information on the graph whether the statement is true or false.

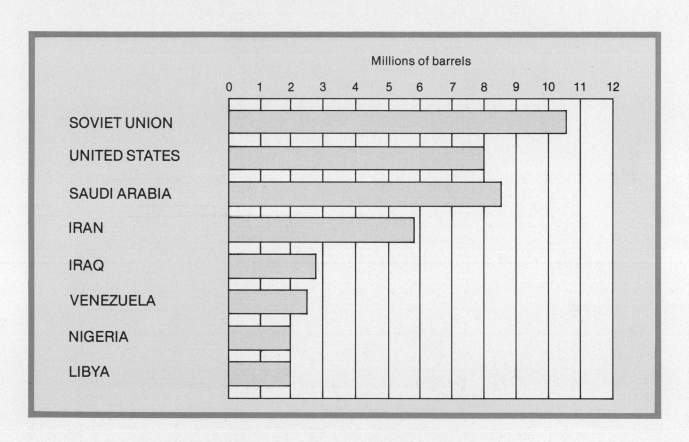

_____ 1. In 1976, the United States was the second leading oil-producing nation in the world.

_____ 2. The Soviet Union has more oil underground than any other nation.

_____ 3. In 1976, the Soviet Union produced over 2 million more barrels of oil than the United States.

_____ 4. In 1976, both Iraq and Venezuela produced more oil than Libya.

_____ 5. Saudi Arabia produced more oil in 1976 than the United States.

_____ 6. The United States produced more oil in 1976 than Iran and Iraq combined.

C. Often bar graphs are used to show a relationship between two ideas, or to compare two related things. Bar graphs can frequently do both of these more clearly than written paragraphs.

Below is a paragraph about United States imports from Africa. Following the paragraph is a bar graph; it gives the same information as the paragraph. Study the graph and the paragraph. Then complete the statements and questions. Write the correct letter in the space provided.

The United States depends on Africa for many of its most important products. Much of the coffee comes from African countries. So does much of the cocoa. In fact, about 40 percent of this product comes from Africa. Without African cocoa, the American chocolate industry would have difficulty staying in business. The United States produces no diamonds. It gets one-third of its diamonds from Africa. It also gets nearly one-third of its platinum from Africa. United States industries also depend on African manganese, chrome, and rubber.

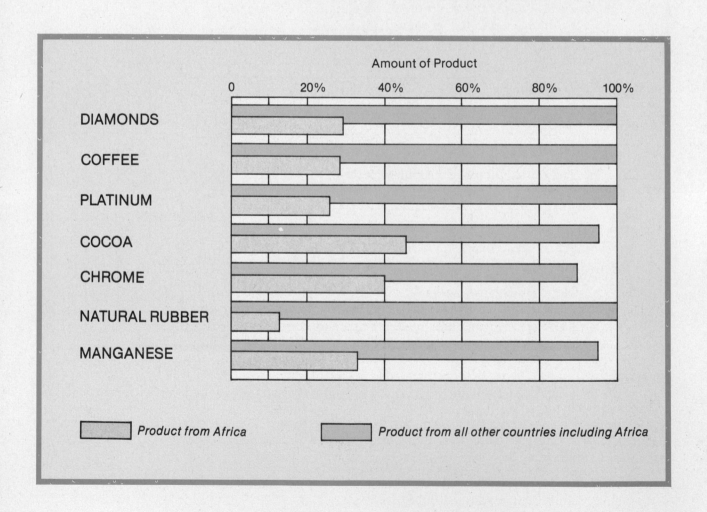

Notice that the graph has two kinds of bars—one light and one dark. The light bars show the percentage of the products the United States gets from all other countries including Africa. The dark bars show what percent of the products come from Africa.

_____ 1. The United States gets 100 percent of which of the following products from other countries?
   a. diamonds   c. chrome
   b. cocoa   d. manganese

_____ 2. African countries supply the United States with the largest percentage of
   a. diamonds   c. natural rubber
   b. cocoa   d. no information

_____ 3. How much of the platinum used in the United States comes from Africa?
   a. 100%   c. 25%
   b. 50%   d. no information

_____ 4. The United States gets more of which product from Africa than from any other part of the world?
   a. coffee   c. manganese
   b. chrome   d. no information

_____ 5. Which of the following products does Africa supply most of to the United States?
   a. manganese   b. natural rubber   c. diamonds

_____ 6. The United States gets about 40 percent of which product from Africa?
   a. diamonds   c. chrome
   b. coffee   d. no information

D. As you learned in the preceding exercise, bar graphs can be used to show the _relationship between parts and wholes_. For instance, the graph showed you what part of all the diamonds the United States uses comes from other countries. It also showed you how much of this part comes from Africa. You saw that the United States gets all of its diamonds—100 percent—from other countries. And you learned that about 30 percent of this amount comes from Africa. The graph pictured the information like this.

	0	20%	40%	60%	80%	100%
Diamonds from all over the world						
Diamonds from Africa						

The graph below shows the relationship between parts and wholes, too. Each bar stands for all the people living in the United States in a certain year. The top bar stands for 1776. The bottom bar stands for 1976.

As you can see, each whole bar is divided into two parts. The parts show you what part of the whole population lived in cities and what part lived in the countryside.

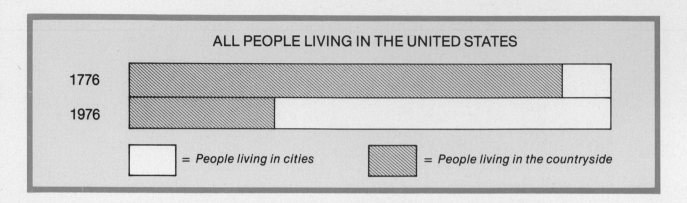

ALL PEOPLE LIVING IN THE UNITED STATES

1776

1976

☐ = People living in cities   ▨ = People living in the countryside

The next bar graph shows what part of all the world's people lived in each continent in 1976. The top bar stands for the whole population of the world in 1976. The bottom bar shows what part of the top bar lived in each continent. Study the graph. Then complete the statements that follow.

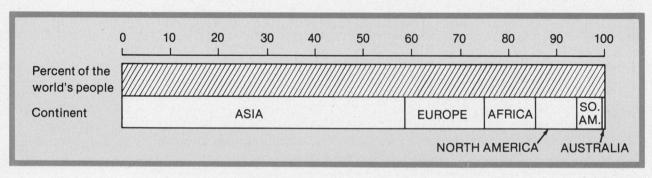

Percent of the world's people

Continent

0 10 20 30 40 50 60 70 80 90 100

ASIA   EUROPE   AFRICA   SO. AM.

NORTH AMERICA   AUSTRALIA

1. _____ contained the largest part of all the world's people in 1976.

2. Asia had about _____ percent of all the world's people in 1976.

3. _____ and _____ had fewer people than North America in 1976.

4. _____ had about 10 percent of the world's people in 1976.

5. Asia had more of the world's people than _____ other continents in 1976.

6. _____ had less than 1 percent of all the world's people in 1976.

70

21. Using Line Graphs

Lesson 21 will show you how to:
- Recognize a line graph—that is, a graph that uses lines to show how things grow in number or size, or increase and decrease.
- Read different kinds of line graphs.

WHAT IS A LINE GRAPH?

A line graph is one that uses lines to show relationships between things. Lines show how things grow in number or size. They also show how things increase or decrease.

The simple line graph below shows how a student's school average improved during the year.

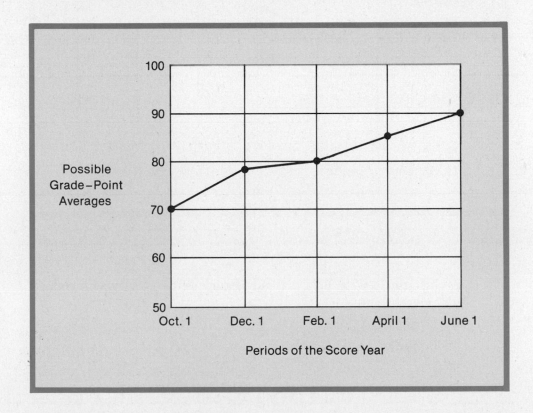

The vertical lines on the graph stand for each two-month period of the school year.

The horizontal lines stand for the grade-point average a student might have.

The diagonal lines connecting the vertical and horizontal lines show how the student's average rose during the year. It went from 70 on October 1st to 90 on June 1st.

WORKING WITH LINE GRAPHS

A. Practice your skill reading a line graph with the one below. Study the graph. Then tell whether each of the following statements is true (T) or false (F). Write an N in the space if you cannot tell from the information on the graph whether the statement is true or false.

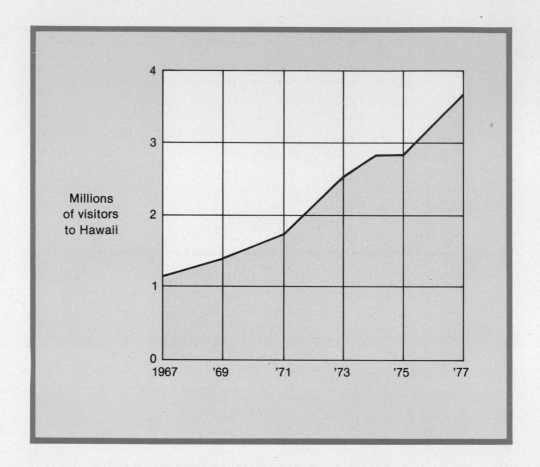

_____ 1. In 1967, there were fewer than one million visitors to Hawaii.

_____ 2. From 1967 to 1977, the number of visitors to Hawaii increased each year.

_____ 3. The line graph shows the number of people who visited Hawaii during a ten-year period.

_____ 4. In 1977, three million more people visited Hawaii than in 1967.

_____ 5. Since the graph shows only the odd-numbered years, we must assume that the even-numbered years are halfway between the vertical lines.

_____ 6. In 1974 and 1975, nearly the same number of people visited Hawaii.

_____ 7. In 1975, the number of visitors of Hawaii passed the three million mark.

B. Line graphs show how things decrease as well as how they increase. Study the graph below. It gives information about deaths caused by automobile accidents. Then tell whether each of the following statements is true (T) or false (F). Place an N in the space if you cannot tell from the information on the graph whether the statement is true or false.

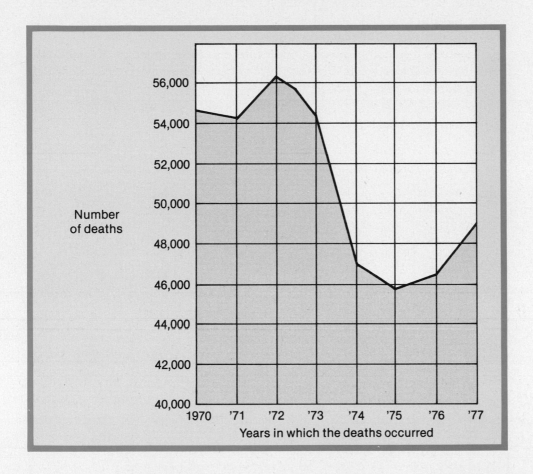

_____ 1. The number of accidental auto deaths has dropped steadily since 1970.

_____ 2. New safety devices on automobiles caused a drop in the number of deaths by accident in 1975.

_____ 3. The sharpest rise in accidental auto deaths took place between 1975 and 1976.

_____ 4. In the last three years shown on the graph, there were fewer deaths by accident than in the first three years shown.

_____ 5. Increased automobile speeds resulted in an increase in deaths between 1976 and 1977.

_____ 6. The greatest decrease in accidental auto deaths took place between 1973 and 1974.

_____ 7. There were about ten thousand fewer accidental auto deaths in 1975 than in 1972.

C. You are now ready to work with a line graph which shows how *two* things are related. Line graphs like this use not one, but two lines to show comparisons.

For instance, if you wanted to compare automobile deaths and airplane deaths between 1970 and 1977, you could add another line to the preceding graph. If you did this, you would also have to make a legend, or key, for the graph. Your key would show which line stood for auto deaths and which one stood for plane deaths.

Here is a line graph that compares the average incomes of black and white families between 1964 and 1976. Look at the key to find out which line stands for black families and which one for white families. Notice, too, that the graph shows only even-numbered years. The odd-numbered years lie between them.

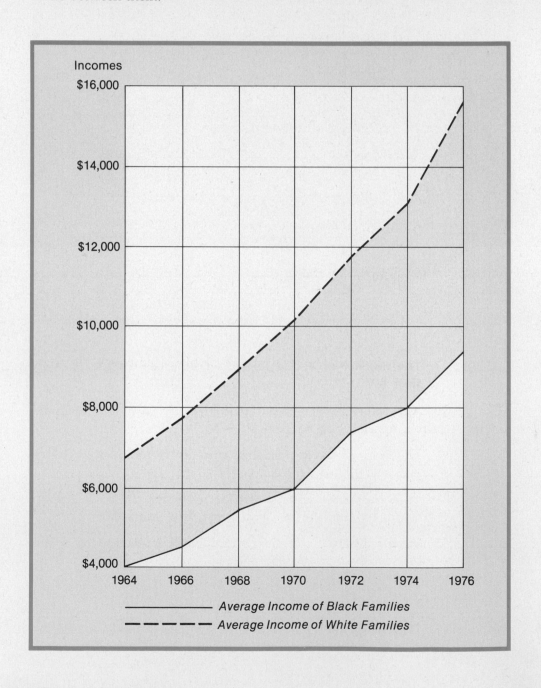

Complete the following statements by filling in the blanks.

1. The difference between the average incomes of black and white families in 1964 was a little more than _____ thousand dollars.

2. The difference between the average incomes of black and white families in 1970 was about _____ thousand dollars.

3. The difference between the average incomes of black and white families in 1976 was about _____ thousand dollars.

4. In 1973, the average income of white families was about _____ _____ thousand dollars.

5. In 1967, the average income of black families was about _____ _____ thousand dollars.

6. The greatest difference between the average incomes of black and white families was in the year _____.

Tell whether each of these statements is true (T) or false (F).

_____ 1. The average incomes of black and white families have increased at the same rate through the twelve years shown on the graph.

_____ 2. The average income of white families grew much more sharply than the average income of black families between 1974 and 1976.

_____ 3. The average income of white families has always been $2,000 more than the average income of black families in the years shown on the graph.

_____ 4. In each two-year period shown on the graph, the average income of black families has increased about $2,000.

D. Now you are ready to use a graph to compare *four* things. Graphs like this look more difficult than others, but they are really not. While they have more lines to study, the graph's legend, or key, tells you what each line stands for.

The graph on page 76 tells about the population of four cities. It shows how the population of each city changed between 1840 and 1977. Each line stands for one city. The years are shown twenty years apart. And the populations are given in groups of 200,000, starting at zero and ending at two million.

Study the graph carefully. Pay special attention to the legend, or key. Then answer the questions that follow.

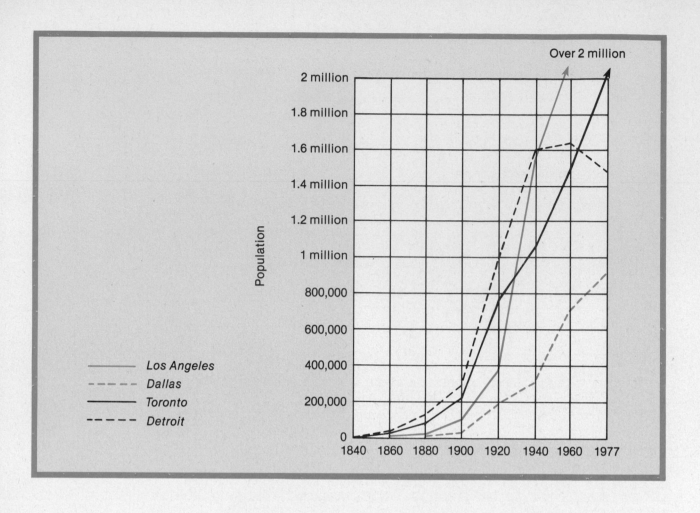

1. Which cities had fewer than 100,000 people in 1860? _____

   _____

2. In what year did Dallas have more people than Toronto? _____

3. When did Los Angeles pass Detroit in population? _____

4. When did the greatest rise in the population of Toronto take place?

   _____

5. In what year did Los Angeles and Toronto have about the same population? _____

6. Which city had the largest population in 1860? _____
   In 1900? _____

7. In 1977, what was the approximate population of Detroit? _____

8. Which cities lost people between 1960 and 1977? _____

   _____

9. What general statements can you make from the information on the
   graph? _____

   _____

22. Circle Graphs

> **Lesson 22 will show you how to:**
> - Recognize a circle graph—that is, a circular-shaped graph that shows the relationship between the whole and its parts.
> - Read several different circle graphs.

WHY DO WE USE CIRCLE GRAPHS?

We usually use circle graphs to show the relationship between a whole thing and its parts. Because the parts of a circle graph look like the pieces of a pie, we often call the circle graph a *pie graph*. The circle stands for the whole pie, or 100 percent. Pieces of the pie stand for parts of the whole. Each one is less than 100 percent.

In this graph, the whole circle stands for all the people who *could have* worked in the United States in 1977, or 100 percent. The large piece stands for the people who *actually did work* in that year. And the small, triangular-shaped piece stands for all the people who did not have jobs in that year.

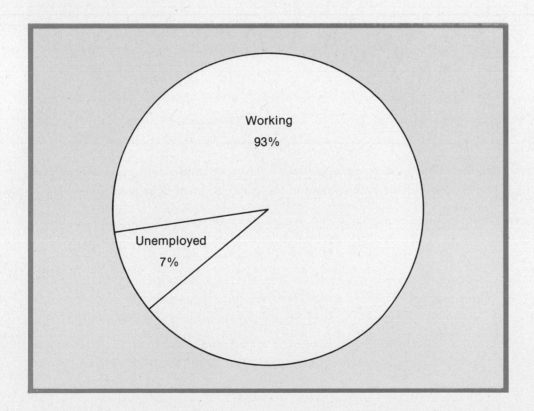

At a glance, you can see that many more people worked in 1977 than those who did not. Even if the graph did not give percentages, the size of the pieces would make the difference clear.

PRACTICE READING CIRCLE GRAPHS

A. The following graphs show where people lived in the United States in 1776 and 1976. Each graph shows how many of all the people lived in the city or the country in one year. By comparing the graphs, we can see how living patterns changed over two hundred years. Remember that the whole circle stands for 100 percent of the people. Study the graphs. Then answer the questions that follow.

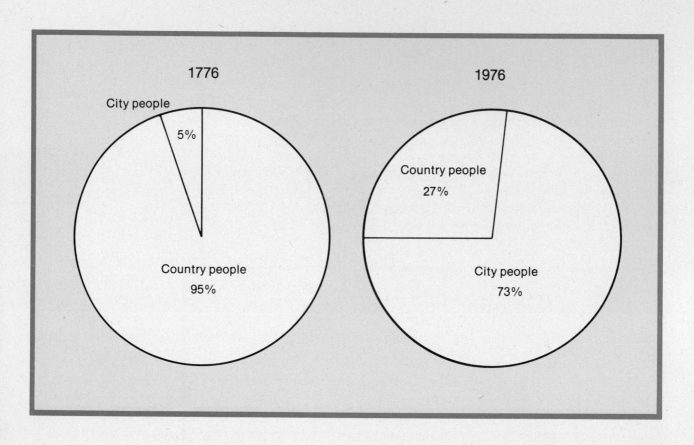

1. What general statement can you make about the change in places where people lived in 1776 and 1976? _____

    _____

2. Compare the circle graphs with the bar graph showing the same information in Lesson 20. Which type of graph shows the information most clearly? _____

3. What general statement can you make about the two types of graphs?

    _____

    _____

4. What percentage of people lived in urban areas in 1776? _____

    In 1976? _____

B. The next graph is divided into three pieces. It shows how much it will cost to control pollution over a period of ten years. Study the graph. Then answer the questions that follow.

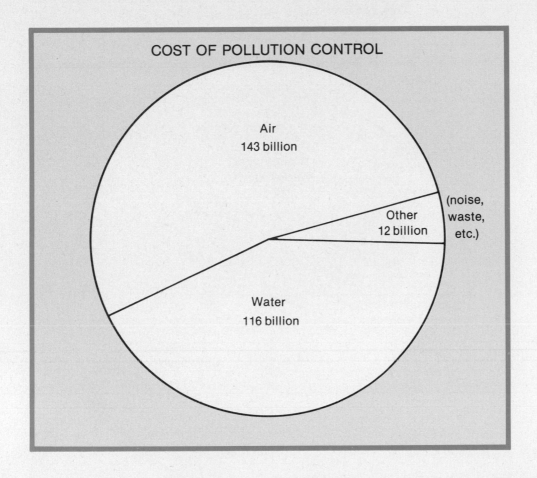

COST OF POLLUTION CONTROL

Air
143 billion

Other
12 billion

(noise, waste, etc.)

Water
116 billion

1. What kind of pollution will be most expensive to control? _____

   _____

   _____

2. Can you tell the cost of controlling noise pollution? _____

   _____

3. According to the graph, what will be the total cost of controlling all

   forms of pollution in the ten-year period? _____

4. Could the graph be divided into more parts? _____

   How? _____

   _____

   _____

   _____

C. The graph below is divided into four parts. It shows the car-owning households in the United States.

Study the graph. Then tell whether each of the following statements is true (T) or false (F). Write an N in the space if you cannot tell from the information on the graph whether the statement is true or false.

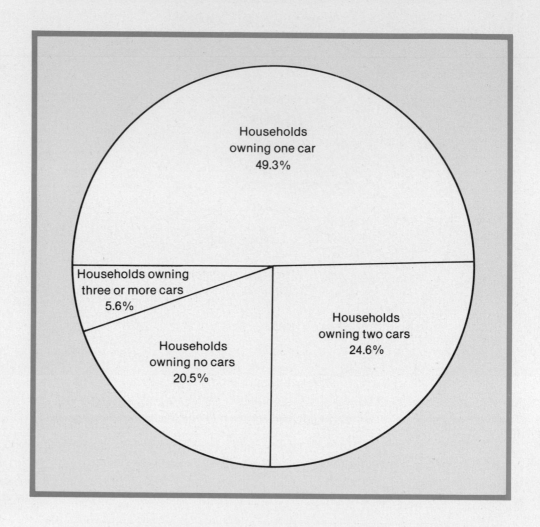

_____ 1. Almost half the households in the United States own one car.

_____ 2. All but five percent of the households in the United States own at least one car.

_____ 3. The graph tells us that no household in the United States owns more than three cars.

_____ 4. More men than women can afford to own cars.

_____ 5. Thirty out of every one hundred households in the United States own at least two cars.

_____ 6. Five out of every one hundred households do not own a car.

_____ 7. More American households have cars than households in any other country.

MAKING YOUR OWN CIRCLE GRAPHS

Now that you have learned how to read several circle graphs, you are ready to make your own circle graphs.

A. Use the information below to make a graph. Your graph should show the average incomes in 1976 of females with seven years or less of school. When you have finished your graph, answer the questions that follow.

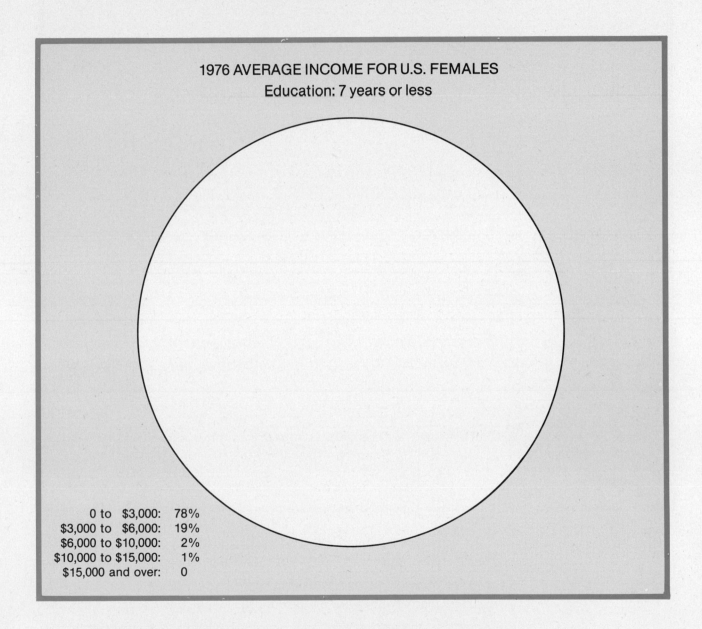

1976 AVERAGE INCOME FOR U.S. FEMALES
Education: 7 years or less

0 to $3,000:	78%
$3,000 to $6,000:	19%
$6,000 to $10,000:	2%
$10,000 to $15,000:	1%
$15,000 and over:	0

1. Which income group had the largest piece of the pie? _____

2. How many women out of one hundred had incomes of more than

   $6,000? _____

3. Which income group did not have a piece of the pie?_____

B. Try your skill again. Make a circle graph using the following information. Your graph should show the average incomes in 1976 of females with twelve years of school.

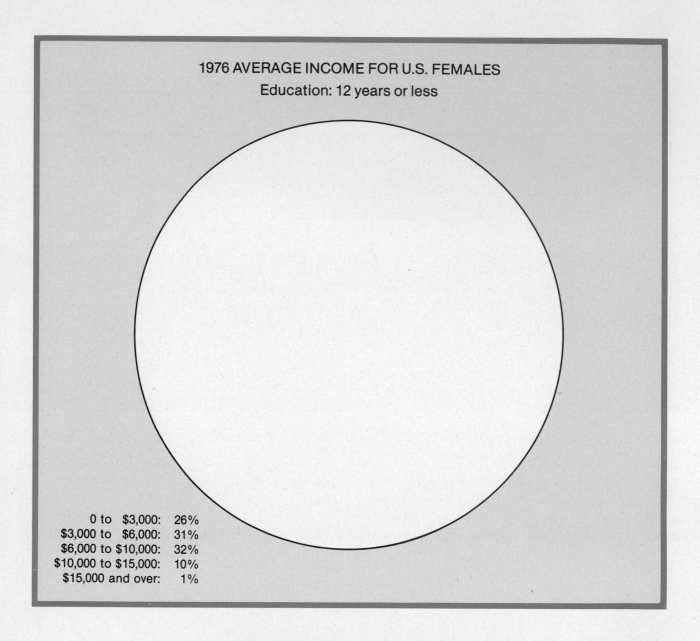

1976 AVERAGE INCOME FOR U.S. FEMALES
Education: 12 years or less

0 to $3,000:	26%
$3,000 to $6,000:	31%
$6,000 to $10,000:	32%
$10,000 to $15,000:	10%
$15,000 and over:	1%

1. Which group had the largest piece of the pie? _____

2. Which group had one-tenth of the pie? _____

3. How many women out of one hundred had incomes of $6,000 or more? _____

4. What does the information on the two graphs tell you about the relationship of education and income? _____

_____

_____

23. More Circle Graphs

> **Lesson 23 will show you how to:**
> • Practice reading circle graphs that are divided into many pieces.

PRACTICE WITH CIRCLE GRAPHS

You are now ready to work with circle graphs divided into many pieces. Each of the circle graphs in this lesson has more than four "slices." In addition, each exercise asks you to work with two circle graphs at the same time. You will study each one and then compare the information on both.

A. The two graphs at the top of page 85 show how the use of energy will change by 1985. In each graph, there are at least five "slices" to study and compare.

   Spend a few minutes studying the graphs. Then tell whether the statements that follow are true (T) or false (F). Write an N in the space if you cannot tell from the information on the graphs whether the statement is true or false.

_____ 1. The graph of 1985 is only an estimate of what the use of energy might be.

_____ 2. The greatest change predicted by the graphs is that there will be greater use of hydroelectric power in 1985.

_____ 3. The graphs predict that the use of oil and coal for energy will drop by 1985.

_____ 4. The graphs show that most places that change from oil to another form of energy will use nuclear power in 1985.

_____ 5. In 1976, solar energy represented less than 1 percent of the total energy source.

_____ 6. The graphs predict that more coal and nuclear energy will be used by 1985 than any other form of energy.

_____ 7. By 1985, coal and natural gas will be the source of nearly half the energy.

_____ 8. The cost of finding substitutes for oil as an energy source will run into billions of dollars by 1985.

_____ 9. In 1976, over half the supply of energy came from oil.

B. The two graphs at the bottom of page 85 show the national budget. They show where the United States national income comes from and how that money is spent. Many individual items have been combined under general headings to make the graphs easier to read.

Study the graphs. Then tell whether each of the statements that follow is true (T) or false (F). Write an N in the space if you cannot tell from the information on the graphs whether the statement is true or false.

_____ 1. Money from social insurance provides most of the income of the national government.

_____ 2. All of the money from individual income taxes could not pay the interest on the national government's debts.

_____ 3. Income taxes from individuals and corporations provide more than half the money for the national government.

_____ 4. The national government borrows money to meet its income needs.

_____ 5. Over 100 billion dollars is spent on national defense.

_____ 6. More money is spent on the health, education, and welfare needs of citizens than for national defense.

_____ 7. More money is spent on aid to cities than on assistance to war veterans.

_____ 8. About ten cents of each dollar of national income is spent for control of pollution.

_____ 9. Fees paid by inventors to register their inventions make up less than 4 percent of the national income.

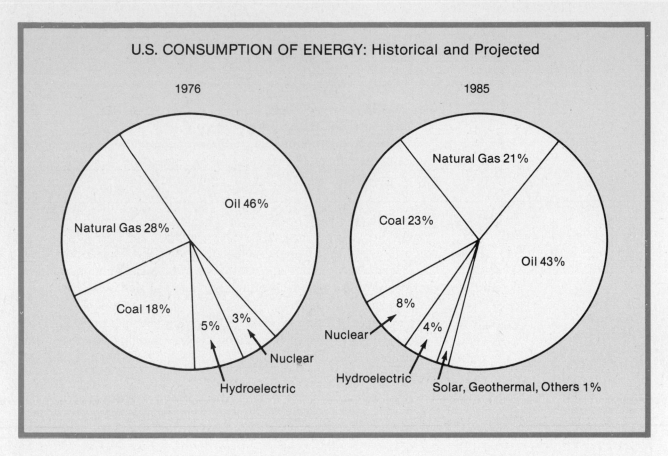

U.S. CONSUMPTION OF ENERGY: Historical and Projected

1976

Oil 46%
Natural Gas 28%
Coal 18%
5%
3%
Nuclear
Hydroelectric

1985

Natural Gas 21%
Coal 23%
Oil 43%
8%
Nuclear
4%
Hydroelectric
Solar, Geothermal, Others 1%

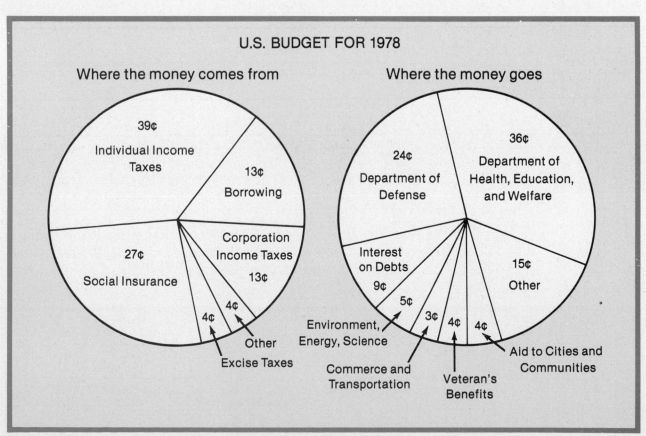

U.S. BUDGET FOR 1978

Where the money comes from

39¢
Individual Income Taxes
13¢
Borrowing
27¢
Social Insurance
Corporation Income Taxes
13¢
4¢
4¢
Other
Excise Taxes

Where the money goes

24¢
Department of Defense
36¢
Department of Health, Education, and Welfare
Interest on Debts
9¢
15¢
Other
5¢
3¢
4¢
4¢
Environment, Energy, Science
Commerce and Transportation
Veteran's Benefits
Aid to Cities and Communities

24. Time Lines

> **Lesson 24 will show you how to:**
> - Recognize the kind of graph known as a time line.
> - Read time lines and construct your own time line.

WHAT IS A TIME LINE?

A time line is a graph that helps us to see the order in which events took place and to understand how they are related in time. A time line is useful in studying the history of the world, of a country, even of our own lives.

A. Below is an example of a simple time line. It covers a ten-year period in the life of Teddy Johnson. Each of the squares on the time line stands for one year in Teddy's life. Study the time line for a few minutes. Then answer the questions that follow.

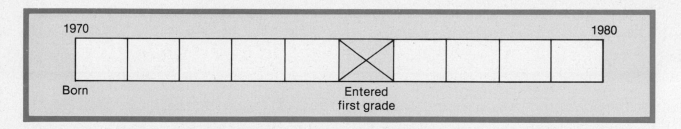

1. When did Teddy enter the first grade? _____

   How old was he? _____

2. Write these dates on the correct squares on the time line: 1972, 1975,

   1978. How old was Teddy in each of these years? _____

   _____

The next time line covers a twenty-year period in the life of Teddy's older sister, Judy. It shows important events in Judy's life. Study the time line. Then answer the questions that follow.

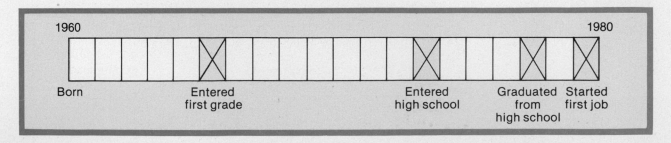

1. What year did Judy enter first grade? _____

2. What year did Judy enter high school? _____

3. What year did Judy graduate from high school?_____

4. What year did Judy start her first job?_____

5. How old was Teddy when Judy entered high school?_____

6. How old was Judy when Teddy entered first grade? _____

7. Write these years in the correct squares on the time line: 1962, 1970, 1975, 1979. How old was Judy in each of these years? _____

_____

B. You are now ready to make a time line showing the important events of your own life. The time line below covers a period of thirty years, from 1960 to 1990. On the time line write at least five important events in your life. If the year of the event is not already on the time line, write it above the correct square. Write the event below the square.

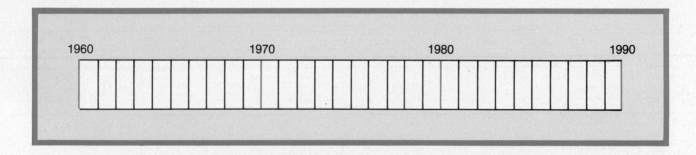

C. The time line below covers one hundred years—an entire century. Because you now understand what a time line is and how it works, we no longer have to use boxes to stand for years. We can use lines instead. Study the time line. Then follow the instructions below it.

1. Place a line where the year 1850 should be. Label it.
2. Place lines where the years 1825 and 1875 should be. Label them.
3. Place lines where the years 1810 and 1890 should be. Label them.

D. Many time lines cover more than one hundred years. The following time line is an example. It covers three hundred years, or three centuries. Study the time line. Then follow the instructions after it.

1700	1800	1900	2000

1. Write the number 1 on the time line where the following years should be: 1750, 1850, 1950.
2. Write the number 2 on the time line where these years should be: 1725, 1825, 1925.
3. Write the number 3 on the time line where these years should be: 1775, 1875, 1975.
4. Write the number 4 where these years should be: 1790, 1890, 1990.

E. Now you are going to read a completed time line. The time line below covers two hundred years, or two centuries. It shows important events in the exploration and colonization of America. Study the time line. Then answer the questions that follow it.

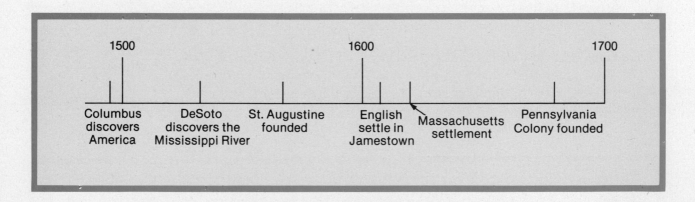

1500			1600			1700
Columbus discovers America	DeSoto discovers the Mississippi River	St. Augustine founded	English settle in Jamestown	Massachusetts settlement	Pennsylvania Colony founded	

1. Which event happened first—De Soto's discovery of the Mississippi River or the founding of St. Augustine? _____

_____

2. Which event happened last—the settlement at Jamestown or the founding of the Pennsylvania colony? _____

3. Which event took place before 1500? _____

_____

4. If you did not know the year in which these events took place, you might be able to estimate it from the time line. Using the time line, write your estimate of the year in which each of these events took place.

   a. Columbus's discovery   _____

   b. De Soto's discovery   _____

   c. St. Augustine founded   _____

   d. Jamestown settled   _____

F. The time lines you have looked at so far have been divided into sections of one hundred years each. The time line below is divided into larger sections, and it covers many centuries. Study the time line carefully. Notice how many years each section covers. Notice how many centuries are shown on the whole time line. Then answer the questions that follow.

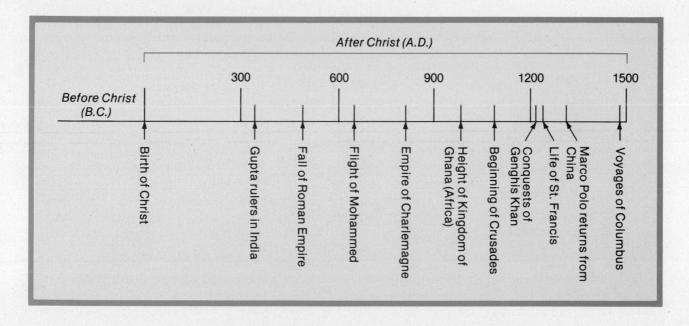

1. Which two people lived at about the same time? _____

   _____

2. Could Charlemagne have met St. Francis? _____

3. How many years passed between the fall of Rome and voyages of Columbus?_____

4. Circle the year that shows when each of the following events took place, according to the information on the time line:

   a. Fall of Rome: 310,   476,   585

   b. Flight of Mohammed: 622,   732,   806

   c. Empire of Charlemagne: 676,   800,   895

   d. Beginning of Crusades: 932,   1095,   1181

G. You will now have a chance to make your own time line of historic events. Study the incomplete time line below. Notice how many centuries it covers. Notice how much time each of the sections of the time line shows.

Next, look at the list of events below the time line. Write the number of each event in the correct place on the time line. Draw a short line below the number to show exactly where the number should go.

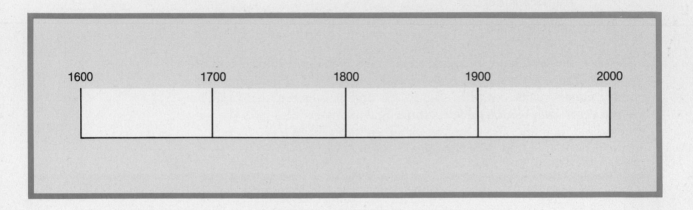

1. 1620: Massachusetts settled
2. 1776: Declaration of Independence
3. 1865: End of the Civil War
4. 1848: Seneca Falls Convention for Women's Rights
5. 1735: Zenger Trial guarantees freedom of the press
6. 1867: Confederation of Canada created
7. 1969: American astronauts land on the moon
8. 1885: Canadian Transcontinental Railroad completed to British Columbia
9. 1939: World War II breaks out in Europe
10. 1954: Supreme Court outlaws segregated schools in America

BEING EXACT ABOUT TIME

Often we use or read expressions that refer to periods of time. Many of these expressions are not exact. As a result, they can be confusing, for not everyone will agree on what they mean. In this lesson, we are going to take a look at some of these inexact expressions. We will see the problems they can create for us when we try to understand time in history.

The expressions on the next page are often used in social studies books. Next to each expression, write the year or years that you think of when you read or hear that expression. When you write the year or period of time that each of these expressions brings to your mind, be as definite as you can. For example, "last year" is a definite time. You know it can refer to only one year. "Several years ago," however, may mean two years to you, ten years to another, and perhaps even more to another. We cannot always understand clearly what "several years ago" means.

1. "many years ago"   _____

2. "in the future"   _____

3. "recently"   _____

4. "a few centuries ago"   _____

5. "in colonial days"   _____

6. "in the Middle Ages"   _____

7. "in the twentieth century" _____

8. "in modern times"   _____

9. "in ancient times"   _____

10. "long ago"   _____

11. "during the period
    of exploration"   _____

12. "in the fifth century" _____

13. "before Christ"   _____

14. "after the Civil War" _____

15. "in the Stone Age"   _____

After you have completed the exercise, compare what you wrote with what your classmates wrote for the same expressions. Are there differences? How great were the differences for each expression?

Can you see why, in the study of history, and in discussions with others, we are asked to remember some dates, or at least to be more definite in our statements about periods of time?

UNIT 4
Research and Thinking Skills

25. How to Use a Table of Contents and an Index

Lesson 25 will show you how to:
- Use the table of contents and the index to locate information in a book.
- Tell if a book will give you the information you are looking for.

THE TABLE OF CONTENTS

When you buy a book or take one out of the library, how do you know if it has the information you want? One way is to look at the book's *table of contents*. The table of contents is at the beginning of the book. It comes after the title page. There you will find the titles of the book's units and chapters and the pages on which they begin. This information will give you an idea of the subjects the book covers.

For example, suppose you are looking for information about the period in history when canals were built. In the library, you find a book titled *The History of Transportation*. This is what you find in the table of contents.

This information tells you that the first part of the book deals with travel by water. The listing of chapters shows that the part about canals begins on page 15. You would probably conclude that the book will contain some of the information you are looking for.

THE INDEX

The *index* of a book is found at the back of the book. Usually it is the last part of a book. It lists the names, places, events, and topics in a book. The list is in alphabetical order, so the exact name or topic you are looking for can easily be located. The list also tells you on what pages in the book you can find the topic you are looking for.

For example, suppose you wished to find out about the life and work of Francisco de Miranda in the history of Latin America. You would look in a book titled, *The History of Latin America*. If you looked in the book's index, you might find a list like this under the "M's":

The list tells you that there are several references to Miranda in the book. They are on pages 121, 122, 123, 124, and 128. Pages 133 to 134 will tell you about Miranda's work with Simon Bolivar.

Remember that the index gives you *particular* information about the contents of a book. The table of contents gives you *general* information about its contents.

USING THE TABLE OF CONTENTS

Here is another example of a table of contents. This one shows the contents of an entire book, not just one unit. It gives us the names of the chapters and the units of the book. And it tells the pages on which each one begins. Study the table of contents for a few minutes. Then answer the questions that follow.

Choose the best answer for each question. Write the letter of the answer in the space provided.

_____ 1. A good title for this book would be
a. *China Today*   b. *Red Flag over China*
c. *A Short History of China*

_____ 2. On what page would you begin reading to learn how China is able to support its large population?
a. 24   b. 38   c. 65

_____ 3. In which unit might you find out how China changed after beginning to trade with other nations?
a. 2   b. 4   c. 6

_____ 4. Which unit might tell you about education in China under a Communist government?
a. 4   b. 5   c. 6

_____ 5. On what page might you begin to read to learn how the Communists won control of China?
a. 39   b. 65   c. 81

_____ 6. In which unit might you find out how rivers have influenced the life of the Chinese people?
a. 2   b. 3   c. 4

_____ 7. Which unit might help you decide whether China will be a world power in the late twentieth century?
a. 5   b. 6   c. 7

_____ 8. On what page might you begin reading about how ancestor worship was a part of Chinese family life for hundreds of years?
a. 10   b. 39   c. 73

_____ 9. On which page might you begin reading about how the Chinese made porcelain and pottery from clay?
a. 24   b. 42   c. 73

_____ 10. Which unit should tell you about the "China that is not Communist" today?
a. 4   b. 6   c. 7

USING THE INDEX

Important Facts About the Index

1. The Index will tell you the pages on which a name or topic is mentioned in a book.

2. If there are several references for the same topic, the references will be in alphabetical order, regardless of the page number. Here is an example:

> Leaders, military, Clark, 77; Gates, 65; Greene, 68; Washington, 59.

Although Washington is mentioned in the book before the others, the listing has his name last in order. This system makes it easier to locate the particular name under the heading of military leaders.

3. Indexes have *cross-references.* Not all information about a topic may be listed under the heading for that topic. For example:

> Agriculture, New England, 56; South, 78. *See also* Farming.

> Farming, Cotton, 62, 78; corn, 66; tobacco, 78, 81. *See also* Agriculture.

A. Here is a sample index. Study the index for a few minutes. Then use the information in the index to answer the questions that follow.

INDEX

Animals. *See* Apes, Hunting
Apes, 9–10, 23, 26, 67
Art, *See* Cave Painting
Caves, China, 22; painting, 13, 20, 48–49; photographs of, 14
Culture, 32–34
Farming, 20, Europe, 65; Fertile Crescent, 51–53; *See also* Tools
Fire, 8, 36, 41
Fossils, 15, 19; Africa, 24; Asia, 26
Hunting, 20, 24; Fertile Crescent, 54. *See also* Tools
Indians, 12; Race, 69, 70
Language, 8, 11, 38, 39. *See also* Writing
Race, 68–69
Religion, France, 45; Germany, 40; Jarmo, 61
Tools, 17–23; Farming, 18; Spears, 19; Stone, 28, 33, 44
Weapons. *See* Tools
Writing, 11, 57

_____ 1. What page might tell you about photographs of ancient art?
      a. 14   b. 22   c. 49   d. not in index

_____ 2. What page might tell you about the ways in which ancient people shaped sticks for farming?
      a. 18   b. 36   c. 65   d. not in index

_____ 3. What page might tell you about animals hunted by people in the Fertile Crescent?
      a. 20   b. 23   c. 54   d. not in index

_____ 4. What page might tell you about the work of the scientist Dr. Davidson Black?
      a. 8   b. 67   c. 70   d. not in index

_____ 5. What page might tell you about the first written language?
      a. 20   b. 45   c. 57   d. not in index

_____ 6. What page might tell you about family life among some ancient people?
      a. 11   b. 32   c. 45   d. not in index

_____ 7. What page might tell you about the shape of bones of some early Asian people?
      a. 23   b. 26   c. 33   d. not in index

8. What might be a good title for this book, judging from the topics in the index ? _____

_____

B. We are now going to look at another index. In this one, there are several page references and topics for each of the items listed. There are several cross-references, too. Study the index for a few minutes. Then use the information in the index to answer the questions that follow.

INDEX

Africa, (map) 161; climate, 162; crops, 162–63; *See also individual countries*

Clothing, 296; Arctic, 302; dependence on climate, 297; industry, 304–06

Coal mining, in Poland, 210; Wales, 166, 176–77; world resources, 208

Explorations, Antarctic, 16; Arctic, 15–16; effect of inventions, 13; to New World, 10–11; routes of, 9–10

Forests, Europe, 220; mid-latitudes, 218; North America, 216; tropics, 216; water supply, 34

Fuels, 159, 421, 463. *See also* Power, Oil

Henry, the Navigator, 11, 24

Lima, Peru, 81, 110; buildings, 81; slums, 82

Oil, 121, 130; Persian Gulf, 321; pipe lines, 132; refineries, 134–36

Pacific Ocean, 76, 77; currents, 421–22; discovery of, 75; explorations, 75–77

Power, from animals, 118; machines, 143. *See also* Fuels, Oil

Rainfall, effect on mountains, 56; effect on people, 54; heaviest, 58–59; winds and, 57

Soviet Union, (map) 144; climate, 146; farming, 147; industries, 149; population in cities, 151; transportation, 152. *See also* Coal mining

Transportation, Australia, 341; Soviet Union, 152; United States, 32

Zambia, climate, 18; herding, 19–20; independence of, 18; minerals, 21. *See also* Africa

_____ 1. What page might tell you if peanuts are grown in Africa?
a. 18   b. 163   c. 216   d. not in index

_____ 2. What page might tell you about Captain Cook's voyages among the islands of the Pacific Ocean?
a. 11   b. 15   c. 76   d. not in index

_____ 3. What page might tell you how the invention of the compass helped in early ocean voyages?
a. 13   b. 16   c. 24   d. not in index

_____ 4. What page might tell you if there is a danger of a coal shortage in the world?
a. 159   b. 176   c. 208   d. not in index

_____ 5. What page might tell you about the coal resources of the Soviet Union?
a. 146   b. 166   c. 208   d. not in index

_____ 6. What page might tell you how animals are used to help irrigate farm lands?
a. 34   b. 54   c. 118   d. not in index

_____ 7. What page might tell you about the kinds of transportation in Zambia?
a. 18   b. 20   c. 152   d. not in index

_____ 8. What page might tell you about the effect of the Rocky Mountains on rainfall?
a. 56   b. 59   c. 216   d. not in index

_____ 9. What page might tell you which countries in the world lead in the manufacture of women's coats and dresses?
a. 296   b. 297   c. 304   d. not in index

_____ 10. What page might tell you about soft woods of the United States and Canada?
a. 32   b. 216   c. 297   d. not in index

C. In a book on American history, would you use the Table of Contents (T) or the Index (I) to answer the questions below? Write either T or I in the space provided.

_____ 1. How many units are there in the book?

_____ 2. Is Thomas Jefferson mentioned in the book?

_____ 3. Where could I find titles of chapters?

_____ 4. Which of these aids is usually in the back of the book?

_____ 5. Which of these aids tells me if there are several references for the same event?

_____ 6. Which of these aids tells me on what pages I could find information about integration in schools?

_____ 7. Which of these aids tells me the page on which Unit 5 begins?

_____ 8. Which of these aids tells me if there is a chapter dealing with problems of farmers?

26. Using Familiar Sources of Information

> **Lesson 26 will show you how to:**
> - Locate the right source of information about a particular subject.
> - Find out more details about a subject that interests you.

HOW DO WE FIND WHAT WE WANT TO KNOW?

Many events and subjects influence our lives. If we wanted to find out more about them, where would we go? How would we begin? How would we locate information about our subject that was accurate and complete? How would we find out if a question had "two sides" and what they were?

Finding Information in Books
Television, radio, newspapers, and magazines can give us some of the information we might be looking for. Books might give us more information about the subject. In school we have all learned how to use almanacs, encyclopedias, atlases, and textbooks.

For many of us, the textbook has become a main source of information. But how do we know which textbook will meet our needs? How can we find the one that will answer our questions?

A. One way we can do this is to learn how to interpret the titles of books. In other words, we can learn how to look at a book's title and know what the title means. For example, each of the following books is about history. But each one will have very different kinds of information. The titles give you clues about what you will find in each book.

   1. *History of the World.* A book with this title would treat the history of peoples of the world over a period of at least 6,000 years.

   2. *History of the United States.* A book with this title might treat about five hundred years of history. The early chapters would discuss nearly the whole world. But most of the book would be about the United States of America.

   3. *North America Since the War of 1812.* This book would cover the last 170 years of North American history.

   4. *The Presidency of Lyndon B. Johnson.* This book would cover a six-year period of United States history. And, for the most part, it would focus on one man.

If a book covers a small amount of time or a small number of subjects, it will probably have major details about one event or topic.

For example, in the preceding list of titles, book number 4 would tell you more about the Johnson administration than any of the books before it. Book 3 would probably treat the Johnson administration in greater length than book 2. And book 1 might treat the Johnson administration in no more than a few lines.

B. Study the following titles. *Circle* the book in each group that would cover the smallest number of topics. *Underline* the book that would cover the largest number of topics.

1. *Government of the United States*

   Indiana State Government

   The Courts of Indiana

2. *World Geography*

   Geography of North America

   Geography of the United States

3. *Peanut Farming in Georgia*

   Farm Products of North Carolina

   Farm Lands of North America

4. *The Colorado River, Lifeblood of the Southwest*

   Waterways of the United States

   Waters of the Western Hemisphere

5. *How to Give Testimony in Court*

   The Constitution of the United States

   Criminal Justice in the United States

6. *History of the Ancient World*

   History of Ancient Greece

   Early European History

7. *Women in America's Work Force*

   History of Labor Unions in the United States

   Women At Work in Factories

8. *Water Travel in the United States in the 19th Century*

   How the Erie Canal Changed New York State

   United States Canals in the 19th Century

Finding Information in Newspapers

Newspapers are full of information. They usually cover almost every topic of interest to us. For instance, most newspapers have:

1. News of world events
2. Local news
3. Sports news
4. Features on cooking, gardening, health care, and similar topics
5. Reviews of movies, books, and plays
6. Announcements of weddings, births, and deaths
7. Editorials—the written opinions of the editors of the paper
8. Columns by well-known writers

Most columns by well-known writers consist of comments on government. Usually these columns appear in dozens of newspapers across the country on the same day. The ideas in these columns are the opinions of the writers. In other words, the writers tell us what they personally think of events in government, in foreign affairs, and in our own society. They do not give us factual, objective reports of the news.

The editors of a newspaper have opinions about the news, too. Their opinions are printed on the editorial page. Editorials are not news items. They are comments on the news. After you have read a newspaper for a while, you can almost predict what the editors will say about a news item.

Each newspaper gives only one editorial opinion about the news. A citizen, therefore, may have to read more than one newspaper to learn different opinions about a particular topic in our society.

Two items that might appear in a daily newspaper appear below and on the next page. The first is a *news article*, or a reporting of facts. The second is an *editorial*, or comments on the news.

A. Read the following news article. Then answer the questions that follow.

CITIES MAKE DO WITH LESS

Today, cities all over the country are finding out that they cannot do many of the things they have done in the past. A decline in the amount of money cities have to spend is the main reason for changes in city life.

Some of the largest cities have been hardest hit by cutbacks in money. They have tried a variety of ways to solve this problem. Chicago stopped its plans for new street lights and street repairs. New York laid off nearly 60,000 workers in a two-year period. Philadelphia closed down its only public hospital. Atlanta cut back on garbage collection and trimmed the food budget for the city zoo. Seattle decided to spend less for trimming grass in its parks and to reduce its street-cleaning force. Others have cut back police patrols and bus routes.

The shortage of money has caused cities to look for new ways to find money. Many city officials feel that tax increases are certain. This has caused protests from citizens in many parts of the country. Help from the federal government has been a source of income. Some city officials feel even more of such help is needed.

1. What is the main idea of the news article? _____
   a. All large cities must increase taxes.
   b. The federal government has helped cities with their money problems.
   c. Cities do not have the money to do the things they want to do.

2. Give three facts or statements to support the main idea of the article.

   a. _____

   b. _____

   c. _____

3. What are some ways to solve the problem mentioned in the article?

   _____

   _____

   _____

   _____

   _____

B. Read the following editorial. Then answer the questions that follow.

CITIES MUST FACE REALITY

Many of the nation's largest cities are calling upon the federal government for help in solving their money problems. This is another case of the "big spenders" asking for the chance to do more of the same. Cities have problems because they have spent money unwisely for years. Now, they are finding there is a limited supply of money for them to spend. City leaders haven't cared much about the poor taxpayers who have given their money for all the cities' spending schemes. Now they find taxpayers cannot or will not give more.

You and I can't spend what we don't have, at least, not for very long. Cities can't either. There are times when we have to "pull in our belts." Cities will have to learn to do the same. We expect our city governments to provide for the health and safety of their people. But they've got to get rid of those things they cannot afford—the new city halls, those fancy music halls, the expensive cars for city officials, the high salaries for city job-holders who do little for the people of the city.

Something has to give. We think it's time for city officials to give something back to their people.

1. What is the main idea of the editorial? _____
   a. Taxpayers want to do away with high salaries for city officials.
   b. If cities have less money, they will just have to cut out the things they can't afford.
   c. Cities should get money they need from the federal government.

2. What arguments are used to support the main idea?

   _____

   _____

   _____

3. Does the news article or the editorial express personal opinions? _____

   _____

4. List three *opinions* stated in the news article or in the editorial.

   _____

   _____

   _____

5. What is the main difference between the news article and the editorial?

   _____

   _____

6. If you wanted to find out facts about the problems of cities, would you

   use the news article or the editorial? _____

7. What reasons would you have for reading an editorial? _____

   _____

   _____

27. Magazines and Encyclopedias

Lesson 27 will show you how to:
- Find the magazine articles that interest you.
- Choose the volume of the encyclopedia that will discuss the topic that interests you.

HOW TO FIND MAGAZINE ARTICLES

Magazines are another good source of information about news events. We call magazines *periodicals* because they come out at certain periods of time—weekly, monthly, twice monthly, and so on.

Like newspapers, magazines can have an editorial "slant." This means that the editors of the magazine can have articles written with a particular view of what is and is not important.

Some magazines specialize. In other words, their articles deal with only certain topics. There are magazines about business, magazines for veterans, magazines that deal with current history, magazines that cover sports, and so on.

To find out what magazines might have information about a topic that interests you, pay a visit to your library. Nearly every library has a *Reader's Guide to Periodical Literature*. The *Reader's Guide* is a listing of articles that have appeared in magazines over a certain period of time. For instance, one volume of the *Reader's Guide* will have articles published in 1976, and another will have articles published in 1977.

In each volume of the *Reader's Guide,* topics are listed in alphabetical order as they are in an index. Look up your topic to find the articles that have been written about it.

A. Here is the way an article would appear in the *Reader's Digest* under the topic heading *Japan*. The information in the box below the sample listing shows you what each part of the listing means.

Japan
New day for trade? T. Nicholson and others. il. Newsweek 91: 53–54
                  Ja 23 '78
(Code for your information:)

Title of the article:	"New day for trade?"
Author:	T. Nicholson and others
il:	illustrated (has pictures)
Newsweek:	name of the periodical in which the article can be found
91:	volume number of the periodical
53-54:	page numbers of the article
Ja 23 '78:	date of the periodical (January 23, 1978)

A plus sign (+) sometimes appears after the page numbers. This means that the article is continued on other pages of that periodical.

B.   Here are some sample entries from the *Reader's Guide*. Study them carefully. Then answer the questions that follow. The listings have been numbered so that you can refer to them easily. Listings are not numbered in the *Reader's Guide* itself.

---

1. *Diet*
    Are we overdoing the diet thing? S.D. Lewis. il Ebony.
    33:43–44+ F '78

2. *Employees*
    Hard work on the way out? interview. E. Ginzberg. U.S.
                News 84: 47–49 Ja 23 '78

3. *Energy*
    Black power; NAACP attacking the proposed energy plan.
         K. Bode. New Repub 178: 12–13 Ja 28 '78
    Energy and the dollar. M. Stone. U.S. News 84: 84 Mr 20 '78
    Facing up to reality. Nat Wildlife. 16: 22–3 F '78
    Jerry-built energy program. il Time 111:28 Ja 30 '78
    U.S. energy demand and supply. R. W. Rycroft. Cur Hist
      74:100–03+ Mr '78

4. *Energy Conservation*
    See Power Resources, Conservation

5. *Engel, George L.*
    Can your emotions kill you? Read Digest 112:133–6 Ap 78

6. *Entertainers*
    Hollywood buzz. il Teen 22:56 Ap '78
    Rock of ages: Christian singers and musicians. P. Baker il
      Sat Eve Post 250:28–30 Ap '78

---

1. Who is the author of an article about Diet? _____

    _____

2. What are the numbers of three listings that have no author named?

    _____

3. How many references are there under *Energy?* _____

4. In what magazine does an article by George L. Engel appear? _____

    _____

5. What is the date of the article in *Ebony* on the subject of diet? _____

    _____

6. Is National Wildlife a weekly or monthly magazine? _____

7. What is the title of an article by M. Stone? _____

   _____

   _____

8. On what page of *U.S. News* is the article entitled, "Hard Work on the Way Out?" _____

9. On how many pages is the article in *Teen Magazine*, "Hollywood Buzz?" _____

10. Which article might tell you how much our use of energy is costing?

    _____

11. Which article might you read to learn about supplies of energy today?

    _____

    _____

12. Under what title would you have to look to find articles about saving energy? _____

    _____

    _____

USING THE ENCYCLOPEDIA

The encyclopedia is another popular and useful reference work. It contains information on a very wide range of topics. In fact, there seems to be no limits to what an encyclopedia can cover.

An encyclopedia usually consists of many volumes. Sometimes there can be as many as thirty. Subjects are arranged in alphabetical order, beginning with A in volume 1 and ending with Z in the last volume.

Because encyclopedias are so big and cost so much to produce, new volumes cannot be published every year. So, be sure to check the date when the encyclopedia you use was published. In this way, you can make sure you are getting the most recent information on a topic.

Practice Working with an Encyclopedia
Each volume of the encyclopedia has a set of *guide words* on the cover. The guide words tell you the first and the last topic in the volume.

This exercise will give you some practice finding topics in an encyclopedia. Study the guide words for each volume shown on page 106 and answer the questions that follow. Write the correct letter in the space provided.

Vol. 1 A to Balloon

Vol. 2 Baltic to Brain

Vol. 3 Brazil to Cleopatra

Vol. 4 Cleveland to Damascus

Vol. 5 Dance to Exchange

Vol. 6 Eye to Guitar

Vol. 7 Gun to Irrigation

Vol. 8 Japan to Marriage

Vol. 9 Mars to Museum

Vol. 10 Music to Perch

Vol. 11 Peter the Great to Railway

Vol. 12 Ram to St. Thomas

Vol. 13 San Juan to Telescope

Vol. 14 Texas to Zoo

_____ 1. If you wanted to know about the most popular breed of dog used in hunting small animals, you would look first in
a. vol. 1   b. vol. 4   c. vol. 5   d. none of these

_____ 2. If you wanted to know about the life of William H. Harrison, president of the United States, you would look first in
a. vol. 7   b. vol. 11   c. vol. 14   d. none of these

_____ 3. If you wanted to know about the Balkan States of south-eastern Europe, you would look first in
a. vol. 1   b. vol. 5   c. vol. 13   d. none of these

_____ 4. If you wanted to know more about a *doubloon*, an old Spanish coin, you would look first in
a. vol. 4   b. vol. 6   c. vol. 12   d. none of these

_____ 5. Where would you look first to learn about the size of Lakes Ontario, Erie, Superior, and the other Great Lakes?
a. vol. 5   b. vol. 6   c. vol. 13   d. none of these

_____ 6. If you wanted to know how gasoline and other products are made from petroleum, what volume would you look in first?
a. vol. 7   b. vol. 10   c. vol. 11   d. none of these

_____ 7. Alfalfa is a plant grown chiefly as food for farm animals in the United States and Europe. If you could not find the information you wanted in volume 1, where else might you look?
a. vol. 2   b. vol. 6   c. vol. 14   d. none of these

_____ 8. A system of printing that enables the blind to read by feeling an arrangement of dots was invented by Louis Braille and named for him. Where would you look first to learn about this?
a. vol. 2   b. vol. 5   c. vol. 11   d. none of these

_____ 9. Great arenas, or stadiums, have been built for bullfighting in Mexico, for soccer in England, and for baseball and football in the United States. Where would you look first to learn how these stadiums have developed?
a. vol. 3   b. vol. 5   c. vol. 13   d. none of these

28. How to Use an Atlas and an Almanac

> **Lesson 28 will show you how to:**
> - Use an almanac and an atlas.
> - Recognize the difference between an almanac and an encyclopedia.

WHAT IS AN ATLAS?

An *atlas* is a book of maps of all kinds. Usually, an atlas includes a map of every nation and territory on the earth. If the atlas is published in the United States, there will be maps of each state and some of the most important cities.

In an atlas, there are also special maps. Among these are Rainfall, Food Production, Vegetation, Voyages of Exploration, Campaigns in Wars, and Religions of the World, to name only a few.

There is also an index that enables the reader to locate every town and city, body of water, and land area on the earth. Places are usually listed with populations as well.

WHAT IS AN ALMANAC?

An almanac is a book of facts. It contains facts about nearly everything you can think of. An almanac will tell you the names and birthdays of all the presidents of the United States. It will contain lists of celebrities like film stars, musicians, writers, and sports figures. In it you will find information about weather patterns, historical events, and many other topics.

Unlike the encyclopedia, the almanac comes out in a new edition each year. So, information is always up-to-date. However, you should still check the almanac's date to make sure you are using the most current edition.

A. Here is part of the index of a leading almanac. The subjects listed are actual topics found in an almanac. Study the listing. Then answer the questions that follow.

Photography	
Awards	404
Inventions	810
Prizes	952
Pierce, Franklin (biog)	305
Pig iron, production	101
Pikes Peak, CO	436
Ping-pong	858
Pinochle	807
Piston champions	886
Pittsburgh, PA	636–39
Buildings, tall	676
Mayor	40
Mileage to other cities	118
Population	192, 218
Pizarro, Francisco (1531)	711
Planets	754–56
Plymouth, Pilgrims (1620)	715
Poe, Edgar A.	360, 671, 688
Poets, noted	358–62
Awards	388
Poland	564
Area, population	564
Cities, population	564
Merchant fleet	110
Petroleum production	90
Polar explorations	430–32
Pole-vaulting records	
Olympic	816
World	860
Poles of the earth	764

1. An almanac gives information about sports and hobbies. Name three of those in this listing.

   a. _____

   b. _____

   c. _____

2. An almanac gives information about the achievements of famous people. Name three in this listing.

   a. _____

   b. _____

   c. _____

3. On which page or pages of an almanac would you look to find the date of discovery of the North Pole? _____

4. On which page or pages of an almanac would you look to find the population of Pittsburgh, Pennsylvania? _____

5. On which page or pages of an almanac would you look to see if Edgar Allan Poe was given an award for his poetry? _____

6. On which page of an almanac would you look to find the oil production of Poland? _____

7. On which page or pages of an almanac would you look to learn the size of the earth in relation to the size of Mars or Jupiter?_____

B. The almanac lists such items as:
1. Awards and prizes of many kinds
2. Buildings—the tallest, largest in area, etc.
3. Cities and information about them
4. Earth and its geographic features
5. Explorations of all kinds
6. Hobbies
7. Mountains and other land features
8. Population of continents, countries, states, cities, etc.
9. Production of minerals, metals, farm products, forests, etc.
10. Records of all kinds
11. Sports, records, and rules

Keep this list in mind as you complete the following exercise.

Read each of the following descriptions of a kind of information. Then decide which reference you would use to find this information—an almanac or an encyclopedia. Write an A in the blank if you would use an almanac. Write an E if you would use an encyclopedia.

_____ 1. The most up-to-date information on the population of a city

_____ 2. The most detailed information about the life of a famous person

_____ 3. The prizes awarded last year for the best writing of popular music

_____ 4. The name of the present mayor of a large city

_____ 5. The greatest amount of information on the operation of the brain

_____ 6. The names of the leading scorers in women's college basketball in the last few years

_____ 7. A listing of the longest bridges in the world

_____ 8. A description of how birds of the jungle are able to protect their young

29. Interpreting Information

> **Lesson 29 will show you how to:**
> - Recognize that even experts on a subject do not always agree.
> - Recognize that everything you want to know about something may not be found in one source.

WHAT'S IMPORTANT?

In this lesson you will see that experts do not always agree on what is important enough to mention in a textbook. Some may think that one detail should be mentioned. Others may feel that another detail is more important.

The following table shows how several textbooks treat four major figures in American history. The table shows how much space each textbook gives to each of the four figures. The facts listed in the table are true. They have been taken from seven history textbooks now being used in junior and senior high schools in the United States. The names of the textbooks have been changed to the names of fictitious authors. These names appear in the column on the far left-hand side of the table.

Here is a description of the abbreviations used in the table:
1. par. = paragraph.
2. col. = columns in a book. (There are usually two columns to a page in a textbook. Each column may have two or three paragraphs.)

Name Textbook	Perry	McCarthy	Carnegie	Sojourner
Albert	1 par.	1 par.	1½ cols.	3 lines
Brenda	2 pars.	0	1½ cols.	0
Charlie	1½ cols.	2 pages	1½ pages	0
Donna	0	1 page	0	4 lines
Edward	0	1 col.	1½ pages	4 lines
Fred	0	0	1 page	3 lines
George	0	3½ pages	0	0

Here is a brief description of each of the four major figures.
1. *Perry:* Commodore Matthew Perry was an officer in the United States Navy. In 1853, Commodore Perry visited Japan. A year after this visit, Japan began to trade with other countries. It began, too, to use the inventions of the modern world.
2. *McCarthy:* Joseph F. McCarthy was a United States Senator from Wisconsin. In the 1950s, he was an outspoken anti-Communist. When he said that many Communists worked in government, the Senate held

hearings to look into the charges. Soon after the hearings, the Senate reprimanded Senator McCarthy because it was shown that his charges were not proven to be true.

3. *Carnegie:* Andrew Carnegie, an immigrant from Scotland, became the leader of the United States steel industry. He was one of the richest people in America. Carnegie gave a lot of money to schools, libraries, and museums.

4. *Truth:* Sojourner Truth, a black woman, was a leading member of the antislavery movement before the Civil War. She also participated in the struggle for women's rights.

1. Which textbook gave the most space to the McCarthy story? _____

   _____

2. Which textbook gave the most space to Perry's visit? _____

3. How many textbook authors felt that all topics were important enough to

   mention? _____

4. How many authors mentioned at least three of the topics? _____

   _____

5. Which textbook author felt that only one of the topics was important

   enough to consider in the book? _____

6. Which topics did most authors feel were important in our history? _____

   _____

7. Which topics did the authors feel were *least* important? _____

   _____

8. One of the topics received less than a paragraph of discussion from each of

   the textbooks. Which one? _____

9. Which of the topics did Brenda feel was most important? _____

   _____

10. Which topic did George feel was most important? _____

11. The topic that Brenda felt was most important was not even mentioned by George. And the topic that George thought was most important was never mentioned by Brenda. How can you explain such a difference in

    opinion between two historians? _____

    _____

    _____

12. How can you explain the fact that in Albert's textbook all topics are at

    least mentioned, while George mentioned only one? _____

    _____

    _____

13. What does the information in this table teach you about the use of one

book for information on a topic? _____

_____

_____

_____

WHICH ONE WOULD YOU USE?

Below are five reference books you might use to find answers to your questions in social studies. Following the list of reference books, there are examples of questions you might wish to find answers for at some time or another. In the blank, place the letter of the reference book in which you would be *most likely to find* a satisfactory answer.

A. almanac   D. *Reader's Guide to Periodical Literature*
B. atlas   E. textbook
C. encyclopedia

_____ 1. Is there a recent magazine article on the subject of pollution in our cities?

_____ 2. What countries in Africa are located on the equator?

_____ 3. What were the arguments for and against the United States taking part in world affairs in the 1920s?

_____ 4. What is the best book to use to find the population of each of the fifty states?

_____ 5. How does Brazil compare in size with the countries near it?

_____ 6. How did printing begin, and how have inventions changed the method of printing to the present day?

_____ 7. What has been written recently about freedom of speech in the Soviet Union?

_____ 8. How many planets are larger than the earth?

_____ 9. Where can you find a short biography of Napoleon Bonaparte?

_____ 10. Which cities of the United States have the tallest buildings?

_____ 11. How much are the governors of our fifty states paid?

_____ 12. What events led to the Boston Tea Party?

_____ 13. What are some large cities that border the Black Sea?

_____ 14. Who wrote the article in *Readers Digest* about making government officials retire at age seventy?

_____ 15. What is a good explanation of geothermal energy?

30. Making a Summary of Your Research

Lesson 30 will show you how to:
- Make a summary of your research by recording the most important points from your written notes.

HOW TO TAKE NOTES ON SOMETHING YOU READ

You must take notes to make sure you remember what you have read or heard. In this lesson, you will learn how to take notes carefully and efficiently.

When you read a selection for particular information, you select the part of the article or report that interests you and that helps you to answer your own questions about a topic. A long article may have only a few parts that help you to find answers to the questions you have prepared. After you have read the selection, do the following.

1. Take each paragraph separately. Find the *main idea or ideas* of the paragraph. Jot them down, using your own words if possible.

2. Think about the reasons why you chose the main idea. Jot down those reasons. These are the *supporting statements.* They prove the main idea. If the statement does not help to prove the main idea you have selected, don't use it.

3. Do this for each paragraph. The main ideas and the statements that support or prove them are your notes. Write your report from these notes, in your own words.

4. The ideas in the selection may have helped you to form some conclusions about the selection. Give your own conclusions or reactions to the selection in your report.

When you have finished your reading, set up the outline for your report like this:

    A. Main Idea, paragraph 1
       1. Supporting statement
       2. Supporting statement
       3. Supporting statement
    B. Main Idea, paragraph 2
       1. Supporting statement, etc.

PRACTICE SUMMARIZING YOUR RESEARCH

On the next page is a magazine article you might read in doing research on the topic "Political Prisoners in the Soviet Union." Following the article is a *list* of possible main ideas for each paragraph and an *outline* of the magazine article to be completed by you.

Read the article carefully. Read it twice if necessary. Then study the list of main ideas. Choose the main idea or ideas that best fit each paragraph. Write them in the correct blanks in the outline on page 115. After each of these main ideas, write supporting statements for them.

Life of Political Prisoners in the Soviet Union

Prison life anywhere is not very pleasant. In the Soviet Union, it is worse than in many places in the world. Most prisoners in the Soviet are sent to labor camps. They are not only sentenced to prison, they are sentenced to hard work. Only a few spend time in prisons as we know them. Many in labor camps are political prisoners. They are called "political" because their crimes are those of speaking or writing unfavorable things about the Soviet government. Others may have spoken out about the treatment of minorities in the Soviet. Probably the most reliable information about the labor camps comes from former prisoners. The Soviet Union does not give information about prisons, the number of prisoners, or their treatment.

Not every prisoner is sent to the same kind of labor camp. If a political prisoner is a first offender, he or she may go to an "ordinary camp." In others, prison life is much more severe. If prisoners say nothing, they can live through the hardships of prison and be freed when their terms are completed. If they speak out for their rights or carry on the thinking that led to their arrest, they can receive even harsher treatment. They can be placed in a dark dungeon away from other prisoners and lose mail and visiting privileges.

In general, those who have spent time in Soviet prisons agree that hunger is the worst torture of the special labor camps. One prisoner reported that the daily meals make a person feel the need for food, and that feeling never ends. Another said that he never ate enough. He could not sleep at night. Yet, he worked eight hours a day under these conditions for five years. Experts who have studied statements of former prisoners believe that keeping people hungry is part of the punishment. Former prisoners say that prison meals would have enough food for a child of nine years of age. On this diet, an adult must do hard labor, and may have to do it for as much as twenty-five years.

Hunger is only one side of the pain found in a labor camp. There are other hardships. A former political prisoner, now living in Israel, said she lived with twenty-three other women in a room ten feet by twenty feet. The women slept in bunks. Each person had one blanket and two sheets which were used as long as a person was in camp. No one had time to wash in the morning. There was one washstand for 120 people. It was possible to take a bath once every ten days. Prisoners could receive a package once every three months. Relatives could visit every fourth month. Of course, if a prisoner dared to question such treatment, these "privileges" were taken away from her.

Possible Main Ideas

First Paragraph:
1. In the Soviet Union there are political prisoners.
2. We know little about prisoners in the Soviet Union.
3. The prison population in the Soviet Union is growing.

Second Paragraph:
1. There are different kinds of labor camps.

2. Prisoners cannot speak out for their rights.
3. There are four kinds of labor camps in the Soviet Union.

Third Paragraph:
    1. Prisoners receive enough food, but it is poorly prepared.
    2. Keeping prisoners hungry seems to be part of the Soviet plan.
    3. Torture is the worst part of labor camps.

Fourth Paragraph:
    1. Visits from relatives give the greatest relief for prisoners.
    2. Political prisoners are given special treatment.
    3. Prisoners are forced to live under inhumane conditions.

Summary-Outline of Magazine Article:

A. Main Idea/s, Paragraph 1

_____

_____

Supporting Statements

1. _____

2. _____

3. _____

B. Main Idea/s, Paragraph 2

_____

_____

Supporting Statements

1. _____

2. _____

3. _____

C. Main Idea/s, Paragraph 3

_____

Supporting Statements

1. _____

2. _____

D. Main Idea/s, Paragraph 4

_____

_____

Supporting Statements

1. _____

2. _____

3. _____

4. _____

31. Generalizations

WHAT IS A GENERALIZATION?

A generalization is a kind of summary of a group of facts. Making one is much the same as making a summary statement, choosing the main idea, or drawing a conclusion.

Generalizations can be correct and incorrect. Incorrect generalizations are usually called "sweeping generalizations" or stereotypes. They are incorrect because they place all persons or things in one category—even when they do not belong there.

For example, it would be wrong to say that "Everyone in my class likes to swim" if some members of your class do not. Yet, many of us fall into the trap of saying "everyone," "all people," "we all know," and similar expressions when they are not true. If you asked your classmates if they liked to swim and most said they did, you could make the generalization that "Most of my class-mates like to swim." But you could not say "all" unless everyone said they liked to swim.

Here are some facts from which you might make a generalization. Study them. Make a generalization. Then compare your generalization with the correct and incorrect generalizations that follow.

The facts
1. London, England, has polluted air.
2. Cities in Germany have polluted air.
3. Tokyo has polluted air.
4. Many large cities in the United States have polluted air.

Correct generalizations
1. Many large cities have polluted air.
2. Many of the world's large cities have polluted air.
3. Large cities on several continents have polluted air.

Incorrect generalizations
1. All cities have polluted air.
2. All large cities have polluted air.

We cannot say, "all" cities from only a few facts. Yet, we can say "many" cities because the facts tell us about many cities in several parts of the world.

Here is another group of facts. You could use these, too, to make a generalization.

The facts

1. Foreigners in ancient Athens were made slaves.
2. Jews were not allowed to be doctors or lawyers in the Middle Ages.
3. Muslims were sent out of Spain because of their religious beliefs.
4. Blacks and Chinese were separated from whites when they came to North America.
5. Mexican immigrants to the United States have had to live in segregated sections of cities.

Correct generalizations

1. Throughout history, people who have been "different" have suffered harsh treatment.
2. History shows us that discrimination has taken place many times in many places.

Incorrect generalization

1. All countries have practiced discrimination in their history.

A. Now you are ready to practice your ability to generalize from facts. Study the facts listed below. Then choose the best generalization for each group of facts. Write the letter of the generalization in the space provided.

>   *The facts*
>   a. In ancient Sparta, boys began training as soldiers at the age of seven.
>   b. In battle, a Spartan was expected to win or die.
>   c. A woman whose son died in battle was the most respected of women.

_____ 1. *Possible generalizations*
>   a. Respect for individual freedom was strong in Sparta.
>   b. Military strength was important in Spartan life.
>   c. The Spartans probably loved stories of adventure and romance.

>   *The facts*
>   a. A shortage of money has caused New York City to reduce the size of its police force.
>   b. Youngstown, Ohio, had to close schools for a time because it could not pay its teachers.
>   c. Lack of funds led Philadelphia to close its only public hospital.

_____ 2. *Possible generalizations*
>   a. Some cities have found they must cut services because of a lack of money.
>   b. All cities in the United States have money problems.
>   c. When there is a shortage of money, cities cut police forces first.

The facts

a. In 1968, there were 8 black members of Congress. In 1978, there were 16.
b. In 1968, there were 40 black mayors of cities. In 1978, there were 163.
c. In 1968, there were fewer than 700 black city officials. In 1978, there were over 2,000.

_____ 3. *Possible generalizations*

a. Blacks have made much progress in the number of elected officials in a ten-year period.
b. Discrimination in voting has been erased from the United States.
c. There were as many black officials as white officials in 1978.

The facts

a. People who are able to work but don't have jobs make up about one-eighth of the poor in the United States.
b. About 8 million of the poor are young people below the age of 16.
c. Several million of the poor are citizens over age 65.

_____ 4. *Possible generalizations*

a. Poor people could improve their conditions if they were willing to take jobs.
b. Most of the poor are in good health.
c. Most of the poor are the very old and the very young.

The facts

a. People in this dry land cannot raise their own food. They buy most of their food from other countries.
b. This land has fertile soil. Almost everything grows well here. Wheat and corn are the main crops.
c. This land is near the sea. The soil is rocky and the growing season is short. Most families fish for a living.

_____ 5. *Possible generalizations*

a. Most people farm for a living when soils are fertile.
b. Geography helps us to decide how people live and work.
c. Most people fish when soils are poor.

B. Read the facts given in each group that follows. Then write a correct generalization for the facts.

1. *The facts*
   a. Philadelphia is a large eastern city with a fine harbor.
   b. Baltimore is a large eastern city with a fine harbor.
   c. Boston is a large eastern city with a fine harbor.
   d. Norfolk is a large eastern city with a fine harbor.

   Correct generalization _____

   _____

   _____

2. *The facts*
   a. The Soviet Union in eastern Europe and Asia is one of the great oil-producing countries of the world.
   b. The United States in North America is one of the great oil-producing countries of the world.
   c. Arabia, in Asia, is one of the great oil-producing countries of the world.
   d. Venezuela, in South America, is one of the great oil-producing countries of the world.

   Correct generalization _____

   _____

   _____

3. *The facts about a North African village*
   a. At certain times during the day, most people stop what they are doing and kneel in prayer.
   b. Many women wear veils over their faces when they appear in the street.
   c. Large numbers of people appear on the streets in modern clothes.
   d. Some farmers use tractors and some use wooden plows pulled by oxen.

   Correct generalization _____

   _____

   _____

4. *The facts about our thirty-eight presidents*
   a. All presidents have been men.
   b. Twenty-nine presidents attended college.
   c. Eighteen presidents have been lawyers.
   d. Twenty-six presidents have come from states with a large population.

   Correct generalization _____

   _____

   _____

5. *The facts about victims of crimes*
   a. Most people who are robbed earn less than $5,000 a year.
   b. Most people whose homes are entered by burglars earn less than $5,000 a year.
   c. Most people who are beaten by others on the street earn less than $5,000 a year.

   Correct generalization _____

   _____

   _____

C. This exercise will give you more practice in making accurate generalizations. Before each of the following statements, write one of these four words: All, Most, Some, No. The word you choose should make the statement an accurate generalization. If you feel you do not have enough information to accurately qualify the generalization, leave the blank empty.

Examples:

No	People have traveled to Mars and back.
Some	People have traveled to the moon and back.
Most	People in the United States own at least one car.
All	Major league baseball teams are in large cities.

_____ 1. City police forces are made up only of men.

_____ 2. Parts of Africa are inhabited by people who live in a jungle.

_____ 3. Farm families in the United States have a more comfortable living than farm families in South America.

_____ 4. Inventions have helped to save lives of people in our country.

_____ 5. Things we learn in school, we will not use in later life.

_____ 6. People in Texas live on large cattle ranches.

_____ 7. Women have been elected president of the United States.

_____ 8. Americans prefer to go to the seashore rather than to the mountains on their summer vacations.

_____ 9. Problems today are worse than they were one hundred years ago.

_____ 10. Ads on radio and TV tell the complete truth about their products.

_____ 11. Rich people work hard.

_____ 12. Black people are rich.

_____ 13. Dogs are larger than cats.

_____ 14. Chinese Americans live on the West Coast.

_____ 15. Trucks are a danger to travelers on the highways.

_____ 16. People should have the right to practice the religion of their choice.

_____ 17. People are sent to prison even though they are not guilty of a crime.

_____ 18. American Indians live on reservations.

_____ 19. Dishonest people are elected to public office.

_____ 20. Puerto Rican people are dark-skinned.

32. How to Supply Proofs for Statements or Generalizations

Lesson 32 will show you how to:
- Give correct proofs for your statements and generalizations.
- Learn to distinguish things that help support a statement from things that do not help to support it.

PROVING YOUR GENERALIZATIONS

In Lesson 31 you learned how to make a generalization from a group of facts. Now you will learn how to support the generalizations you make with correct proofs.

Following are some examples of generalizations. Each generalization is followed by a list of statements that could be used to prove it. In each list, several statements may be correct proofs for the generalization. Study the generalizations and the proofs carefully. Notice which proofs are correct and why they are.

1. *Generalization:* Our school basketball team was the best in the city last year.

   Possible Proofs (Supporting Statements)
   a. Our team won twenty games and lost two—the best record in the city.
   b. Our team defeated every other section leader during the year.
   c. Two of our players scored more than three hundred points during the season.

   Reasons a and b support the statement that the team was the best in the city. They had the best record and defeated all other section leaders. Reason c *does not* help to prove the statement. Because two players had good scoring years does not prove that the team was the best. It just shows that two players had good seasons.

2. *Generalization:* Iris is a very popular girl with her schoolmates.

   Possible Proofs
   a. She was elected captain of the basketball team by her teammates.
   b. She was elected president of her class.
   c. She was appointed a lunchroom monitor by the principal.
   d. She has made the honor roll this year.
   e. She attends nearly all social events in school.
   f. Iris is always in the middle of a group in the school yard.
   g. She is the first one chosen when sides are picked in gym classes.

Reasons a, b, f, and g all support the statement that Iris is "popular." Her schoolmates chose her as a leader and like to be in her company. Reasons c, d, and e *do not* support the statement. The principal, not her classmates, chose her to be a monitor. The fact that she goes to school affairs does not tell us that she is liked. The fact that she has achieved honors tells us that she is bright, not necessarily that she is popular.

PRACTICE FINDING PROOFS

You will now have a chance to practice finding proofs for generalizations. Read each of the following generalizations. Then read the list of proofs after it. Choose the proof or proofs that support each of the generalizations or statements. Write the letters of the correct supporting statements, or proofs, in the blanks before each generalization.

1. The people of the United States enjoy more home conveniences than any other people in the world.

   Possible proofs:
   a. There are more than 215,000,000 people in the United States.
   b. Eight out of ten families in the United States own at least one car.
   c. Almost every home in the United States has at least one TV set, and three out of four have color TV.
   d. The United States government has set aside thirty-six national parks for recreation and leisure.

2. In the last fifty years, the eating habits of Americans have changed.

   Possible Proofs:
   a. Cereals are the favorite breakfast food of Americans.
   b. Americans eat twice the amount of chicken they ate fifty years ago.
   c. Americans have always liked vegetables with their meals.
   d. Americans eat half the eggs they ate in 1925.

3. Good medical care has become a serious problem in the United States.

   Possible proofs:
   a. On the average, American men and women can look forward to longer lives than ever before.
   b. Good medical care has become expensive.
   c. There are many older people who are in need of medical care, but who have little income to pay for it.
   d. Young people are vaccinated against smallpox and polio.

4. Geography helps to decide where and how people live and work.

   Possible proofs:
   a. People in crowded islands often fish for a living.

b. Akron, Ohio, has been the center of the rubber industry because Charles Goodyear made his discoveries about processing rubber there.

c. Some people in dry lands take tents and animals with them as they move in search of water.

d. The people of some countries are largely farmers because there are few mineral resources in their land.

5. Humans seem to want more than those things that are easily available to them.

Possible proofs:

a. The United States has enough coal resources to meet its needs.

b. The United States imports rubber, oil, and pepper from other countries.

c. The United States was once torn by a Civil War between the North and South.

d. European nations carried out voyages to Africa, India, and America in the fifteenth and sixteenth centuries.

6. Japan must trade with other countries in order to get food for its people and materials for its industries.

Possible proofs:

a. Japan has a large population living on a crowded series of islands.

b. Most islands in Japan are mountainous. There is little farmland.

c. The Japanese people are alert, hard workers.

d. Japan has almost none of the oil, rubber, and iron it uses in manufacturing.

7. Immigrants to the United States have contributed to the growth and wealth of the nation.

Possible proofs:

a. Many immigrants from Europe settled in eastern cities.

b. Immigrants from many nations settled in those parts of cities where there were people of the same nationality and language.

c. Chinese workers helped to build railroads in the West.

d. Andrew Carnegie came to this country from Scotland and became a leader in the steel industry.

8. The ancient Greeks made great discoveries in mathematics and physics.

Possible proofs:

a. Greek plays were acted in outdoor theaters.

b. Archimedes explained the principle of the lever to move heavy objects.

c. Euclid set down the principles of geometry.

d. Hippocrates is known as the Father of Medicine.

_____ 9. The problem of pollution is worldwide.

_____ *Possible proofs:*
   a. Smog hangs over cities in North America, England, Germany, Japan, and the Soviet Union.
   b. Some American cities are running out of space to dispose of garbage.
   c. Art works are being ruined by chemicals in the air.
   d. Lake Erie in the United States, Lake Baikal in the Soviet Union, the Ganges River in India, and the Rhine River in Germany are a few of the bodies of water that have been polluted.

_____ 10. The invention of the automobile has been a blessing and a curse.

_____ *Possible proofs:*
   a. Many families in the United States have at least two cars.
   b. Thousands are killed in automobile accidents each year.
   c. Thousands of new jobs were created in making, repairing, and servicing automobiles.
   d. The auto has been the chief means by which people have been able to travel during their vacations.

_____ 11. Religion was an important part of the lives of ancient people.

_____ *Possible proofs:*
   a. Egyptians lined their temples with statues to please their gods.
   b. The Hebrews developed a religion based on the belief in one God. Their religion was their law.
   c. The Incas developed a great civilization high in the mountains of South America.
   d. The Phoenicians developed an alphabet that is the basis for our own alphabet.

_____ 12. A good education is more important in the United States than ever before.

_____ *Possible proofs:*
   a. Education helps people of different backgrounds to live together in peace.
   b. More books are published each year than ever before.
   c. People without skills and training cannot find good jobs.
   d. There is a growing demand for unskilled workers.